Swaddle Me Up

Meleah Ekstrand

photographs by **Bill Milne**

illustrations by **Kat Yao**

dle
Me Up

**Baby Wrapping
and Babywearing for Everyone**

CHRONICLE BOOKS

SAN FRANCISCO

ISBN 978-1-7972-0729-2

Manufactured in China.

Design by Vanessa Dina.
Typesetting by Frank Brayton. Typeset in Sofia Pro.
Photographs by Bill Milne.
Illustrations by Kat Yao.

Baby K'Tan is a registered trademark of Baby K'tan, LLC. Beco is a
registered trademark of Boba, Inc. Boba is a registered trademark of
Baby Earthling, LLC. Didymos is a registered trademark of Erika Hoffman.
Ergobaby is a registered trademark of The Ergo Baby Carrier, Inc. Girasol is
a registered trademark of Girasol GbR. Infantino is a registered trademark
of Blue Box Opco, LLC. Kinderpack is a registered trademark of Melissa-
made, Inc. LÍLLÉbaby is a registered trademark of LÍLLÉbaby, LLC. Moby
Wrap is a registered trademark of Baby Bella Maya, LLC. Natibaby is a
registered trademark of SPESAR Sp. z o.o. sp.k. Sakura Bloom is a registered trademark of Sakura Bloom, LLC. Solly Baby is a registered trademark
of Solly Baby, Inc. WildBird is a registered trademark of Wildbird, LLC. Wrap
Your Baby is a registered trademark of Wrap Your Baby.

The information contained in this book is presented for educational
purposes only. This book is in no way intended as a substitute for the
medical advice of physicians.

10 9 8 7 6 5 4 3 2 1

Chronicle books and gifts are available at special quantity discounts
to corporations, professional associations, literacy programs, and
other organizations. For details and discount information, please
contact our premiums department at corporatesales@chronicle-
books.com or at 1-800-759-0190.

Chronicle Books LLC
680 Second Street
San Francisco, California 94107
www.chroniclebooks.com

Dedication

To my husband, Neal, for fully supporting every endeavor I have ever embarked on. Thank you! And to my kids, Emmett, Westin, Cole, Cielle, and Miles, you made me a mother, and I am forever grateful for each one of you.

Introduction 8

Swaddling

Why Swaddle? 13

Swaddling Historically 15

Swaddling Basics 16

When to Swaddle, When to Stop 17

Can You Swaddle Too Much? 19

Avoid Swaddling Pitfalls 21

How to Swaddle

Good-Enough-to-Eat Swaddle 23

Can't-Break-Free Swaddle 27

Quick-and-Easy Swaddle 31

The Let-It-Hang Swaddle 35

One Arm In, One Arm Out Swaddle 39

The Blowout Swaddle (sweatshirt) 45

Bathtime Swaddle 49

Too-Tired-to-Care Swaddle 53

I-Got-You-a-Present Swaddle 57

Sweet Pea Swaddle 61

Babywearing

Why Babywear? 69

Babywearing Historically 70

ABCs of Babywearing and Safety 72

Check Your Fit 77

Types of Carriers for Babywearing 78

  Ring Sling 79
  Stretchy Wrap 81
  Woven Wrap 84
  Soft Structured Carrier (SSC) 87
  Meh Dai (also known as mei tai) 90

How to Babywear

  How to Wear a Ring Sling on Your Front:
    Heart-to-Heart Hold 100
  How to Wear a Ring Sling on Your Hip:
    Ring Sling Hip Carry 104
  How to Wear a Stretchy Wrap:
    Heart-to-Heart Hold 108
  How to Wear a Woven Wrap:
    Front Wrap Cross Carry (FWCC) 114
  How to Wear a Soft Structured Carrier: Facing In 120
  How to Wear a Soft Structured Carrier: Facing Out 124
  How to Wear a Meh Dai: Heart-to-Heart Hold 128

Back Carrying 132

Resources 138
Index 140

Is there anything better than a warm, snuggly baby on your chest? Combine those snuggles with that new-baby smell, and it's a wonder new parents would ever want to get up from their snuggle spot. Alas, showers still need to happen, food must be eaten, and the occasional dish has to be washed. But wait, that sweet baby snuggled on your chest is very unhappy when they are laid down. Or maybe you have a newborn who isn't snuggling so much and is doing more crying—also totally normal. Faced with these scenarios, what is a new parent to do? Welcome to the world of swaddling and babywearing, your new best parenting friends.

My goal in this book is to help you find the right tools to enjoy this stage a little more and, for those moments when none of those tools works, provide you with a little humor to get through this phase in life. Because, let's be honest, no matter what you do, or how amazing you are at caring for your little one, or how awesome the advice in my book is, babies have bad days; sometimes all we can do is laugh and try again tomorrow.

I gave birth to my first child in 2010. It was love at first sight. Before I knew it, I realized I didn't just love newborns, I loved everything about babies—birth, breastfeeding, babywearing. OK, maybe I didn't love it all right away; there was definitely a learning curve for lots of it. I found myself scouring websites and books at night trying to figure out when we needed to stop swaddling (because my baby loved it and I didn't really want to stop), how to wear a baby carrier, and which one to buy. Despite the difficulty, I found that I thoroughly enjoyed being a new parent and I loved sharing information that I had learned with friends so they didn't have to spend the same number of hours scouring websites and books looking for the information. In fact, I spent many nights in a chair, snuggling my baby to my chest as I read and searched for the parenting information I was looking for. Eleven years later, I've had four more babies and become a birth doula, newborn and childbirth educator, breastfeeding support provider, and babywearing educator. Helping other families navigate this journey has become what I love to do.

Over these past 11 years, as I have taken care of my own babies and supported many families through their journeys in parenthood, I have learned a few things. One is that not everyone loves this newborn stage, and that is OK. Or you may love lots of things about it but still find you need more information in order to understand and enjoy your baby better. That is OK too.

If I know one thing about babies now, it's this: After 9 months of feeling safe and secure, they want to replicate that feeling, and swaddling and babywearing help them feel safe and secure. This book will teach you the art of swaddling, why we do it, how to do it, when to do it, and when to stop. You will learn different ways to swaddle and a few funny swaddle ideas as well—humor is definitely important to maintain as you embark on this journey of parenting. Swaddling keeps many babies happy and secure, especially in those early months; often, as the baby gets older and ages out of swaddling, you may find you have a baby who's desperate to hang out with you all the time, and your arms are tired. Babywearing to the rescue. Babywearing provides a comfortable place for your baby to hang out and be happy, maybe even take a snooze while you get some things done or just take the opportunity to watch a show in peace. This book is going to teach you the ABCs of babywearing, ways to check if your baby is being worn safely, how to decode the different types of carriers, and how to put your baby in a carrier. Babywearing can create an amazing sense of freedom that you haven't felt since before your baby was born.

I will close this introduction in the same way I finish all the classes that I teach. *You* are the expert on your baby. *You* know better than anyone what they need, what they like, and what is best for them. You may not always know right away; it may take some time to learn what it is they need or want (and that's OK!), but you are the one that spends day in and day out with them, and you know your baby best. Please take the advice in this book that works for you and your family and leave the rest! Most babies love swaddling and most babies love babywearing, but just as we all have different personalities, so do babies. Try what works for you in this book and move on from what doesn't!

Swaddling

Why Swaddle?

Have you ever gone somewhere new and felt completely out of place? Now imagine that you have no voice to express your discomfort. Maybe you are cold and forgot your jacket, or that warm sunny day is quickly turning chilly as the sun sets (we have all been there! OK, everyone except for my husband, who is constantly hot; we will consider him an outlier). You might feel like you want to cry, but you won't because you are an adult and have some ability to control your emotions. Now you have a small idea of what your little one is going through, and they certainly are not able to control emotions yet. This cold new world is pretty shocking for your baby, who once felt completely safe, secure, and warm inside the womb. Swaddling helps your baby get back to that safe world, and when your baby feels safe and comfortable, they are happier, and that means no more crying (or at least less crying). Swaddling is a great starting point to help your baby feel secure and happy.

Babies spent 9 months in a very confined space, where they were constantly fed and rocked to sleep as mom walked around, and then birth happened and they were introduced to hunger, fluctuating temperatures, a wet diaper, separation, and the inability to help themselves with any of those issues. It really is rough to be a baby! They have also learned that their legs and arms can extend a lot more than before, and they aren't always in control of what's happening to their limbs. On top of all that, babies are born with what is called the Moro reflex. It is aptly nicknamed the startle reflex because when babies are surprised by a loud noise or a bright light or who really knows what, they throw their arms, and often their legs, up into the air, startling themselves awake! The Moro reflex happens when babies are on their backs. Now if you have had your baby for even a few short days, you may have picked up on the fact that your baby sleeps happily lying heart-to-heart on your chest, but as soon as you lay them down on their back, they wake. Thanks, Moro reflex! So, to avoid the Moro reflex, why don't you just transfer your baby from your nice warm chest to a crib still lying on their tummy? Unfortunately, babies who sleep on their tummies are at a higher risk of SIDS (sudden infant death syndrome), and putting your baby to sleep on their back reduces the risk of SIDS by 40 percent. (To learn more about SIDS, see page 15, Swaddling Historically.) You're

now learning that the age-old metaphor "sleep like a baby" really means nap 10 times a day for 20 minutes, and not sleeping deeply for several hours, which is what you thought it meant. Swaddling helps your baby deal with all these things—helps them to feel warm, cozy, and contained, and to not startle awake, since their arms and legs are held in by the swaddle. This way you can finally take a bite of food while it's still warm or rinse all the shampoo out of your hair during your shower. And, of course, the baby can finally get some good sleep!

Some might be a little put off by swaddling, feeling that their baby needs freedom! I get it, but the truth is that babies generally like to be swaddled, even if they protest during the transition from unswaddled to swaddled. Take a screaming, crying, flailing baby, wrap them up tight, and watch as the screaming, crying, and flailing stops. If your baby truly doesn't like to be swaddled, that's OK too, but for those babies who love it, why should we deny them?

Swaddling Historically

Humans have been swaddling their babies for centuries: The ancient Greeks and Romans swaddled their babies, as did European peasants in the Middle Ages. From one culture to another, and over different eras in history, swaddling has been done in many different ways, using different fabrics and for different reasons, to wrap up a baby. Some used it for sleep, some to keep them warm and calm, and some to "shape a child's body." In the 1700s, things changed. Parents, spurred on by the French and American revolutions, decided to free their

children from the "bondage" of swaddling. Swaddling was too confining; never mind that it helped calm the baby, kept them warm, or encouraged sound sleep.

So what changed from the 1700s freedom movement to now? Well, things actually started to change in the United States around the 1990s, when the Back to Sleep campaign rolled out. Babies were dying of SIDS, and it was discovered that by putting babies to sleep on their backs, alone in a crib or bassinet with no loose blankets or clothing, the SIDS risk was reduced by 40 percent. Those statistics are really compelling, but as many have already figured out, babies don't particularly like to sleep on their backs or on their own. Over the decades, it's become important to help parents figure out how to help their babies sleep better while also keeping them safe. Of course, one option that can work for your family is to safely co-sleep (to learn more about safe co-sleeping options, visit https://cosleeping.nd.edu). But for many parents, this isn't the right option, or even if it is, they need a way to help their baby sleep safely alone sometimes, even if it's just for a nap. But how do you get your baby who refuses to sleep safely on their backs to sleep alone in their crib? Bring back the swaddle!

Swaddling Basics

- Square blankets are best.

- 44 by 44 inches [112 by 112 cm] is an ideal size for most babies aged newborn to 4 months.

- Cotton and muslin are ideal fabrics to use since they are thin and breathable. If you live in a cold climate and your baby will be swaddled in a stroller (not being worn in a baby carrier, where they will share body heat with you), you can use a blanket such as a fleece or a quilt to help keep them warm. Or you can dress them more warmly inside the swaddle.

- Swaddled babies should always be laid down on their backs, never on their tummies.

- When you swaddle your baby, you want the blanket to be taut but not tight. It is taut enough if you can just slide your hand between the baby's chest and the blanket.

- Swaddling is most easily done on a soft, flat surface such as a bed, couch, or carpeted floor.

- Don't be discouraged if your baby resists or cries when you start swaddling—they aren't aware of the bliss that is about to come. Just swaddle your baby and then take up to 5 minutes to rock and shush them. If your baby gets more upset or does not seem to be settling, unswaddle and see if your baby needs something else, like a feeding or a diaper change.

- To prevent your baby from breaking free from their swaddle, make sure their arms are straight down by their sides. Bent arms that are swaddled are able to break free.

When to Swaddle, When to Stop

How soon can you start swaddling? Basically, you can start within the first few hours after birth. Of course, in those first few hours you want to soak up all the cuddles and skin-to-skin time with your new baby (see page 19 for more about skin-to-skin). But no one can hold their baby 24/7, and that's where swaddling (and babywearing, which we will talk more about later) comes in. So don't hesitate to do skin-to-skin for as long as you need or whenever you want; but when you need a moment to yourself, to rest your arms, or to take a shower, it's never too early to swaddle.

Your baby was born, skin-to-skin was great; your baby has been happily swaddled for months now. So when do you stop? Swaddling your high schooler sounds good, right? I mean, why stop a good thing? The short answer is, you stop swaddling when your baby learns to roll over. It is no longer safe to swaddle your baby if your little gymnast has learned to roll from belly to back or back to belly. This can happen as early as 2 to 3 months but is more typical at 4 to 6 months. The long answer, though, is that some babies don't learn to roll for a while but still are done being swaddled. If they are constantly playing Houdini and trying to break free from the swaddle, or if the swaddle seems to no longer calm them but instead frustrates them, they are ready to move on from swaddling. But, you may say, my baby Houdini'd out of the first swaddle I tried, or has been fussing from day one, or is having a growth spurt and isn't so keen on the swaddle while that's happening. With most things in parenting, my advice is to give it about 5 days. If your baby is always unhappy with swaddling or happier once they have broken free, it is probably time to end this practice. Remember: You are the expert on your baby, and if you have given it a good solid try and your baby seems happier not swaddled, don't second-guess yourself. Trust yourself and trust your baby.

But even if your baby still loves swaddling, all good things must come to an end. When it is time for swaddling to stop, there may be a transition period. If your baby happily moves on, run with it; but if they seem to be struggling to say goodbye (and maybe you are as well!), you can try to help that transition by first just swaddling one arm in and one arm out (see page 39). After a week or two of one arm in, one arm out, try no swaddle at all and switch to a sleep sack. Some babies transition easily with this slight assist and are happy to move on from the swaddle. Others are what I like to call "higher needs"—these babies really thrive on connection, contact, and being held. They may need some extra snuggles and a lot more babywearing as they transition out of swaddling. But don't worry, they all transition to the next phase, even if there may be some resistance. That's OK; parenting is not about having our child avoid hard things but helping them navigate hard things. You have got this and so has your baby.

Can You Swaddle Too Much?

A baby who is swaddled is happy, content, and likelier to sleep better. There is no way there could be too much of a good thing, is there? Actually, there is: Babies can be over-swaddled. Babies who are swaddled do sleep well, and sometimes too well. Some babies, I like to call them "happy-to-sleep babies," really like to sleep and choose to do that instead of waking up to eat. (Maybe it's an inherited trait from one of their parents? I'm not pointing any fingers!) Newborns should be eating a minimum of 10 to 12 times in a 24-hour-period. A swaddled newborn baby (less than 3 weeks old) who is choosing to sleep longer than 3-hour stretches and is not waking up to eat is being swaddled too much.

Hold Your Baby Skin-to-Skin!

As soon as your baby is born, get that connection and bonding started by cuddling skin-to-skin. This contact is shown in many studies to strengthen the bond between baby and parents. In addition, it can help a new baby regulate their temperature and breathing, which some new babies can struggle with as they transition to the outside world. It also makes your little one cry less, as they are comforted by you! There are benefits not only for the baby, but also for the parents. Parents who do skin-to-skin early and often report better bonding with their baby and reduced postpartum depression. It's a great way for parents to connect with their new baby. So snuggle that baby right away and as often as you like. Let me emphasize that—you cannot hold your baby too much!

You may enjoy the extra hours of peace and quiet, but your baby is at risk of not gaining enough weight as a result of so much sleep. Weight is a pretty important factor in baby growth and development. Babies who are gaining weight at a certain pace tend to be happy babies who hit their developmental milestones. If your baby is not waking at least every 3 hours at night and ideally about every 2 hours during the day, it will be very hard to fit in the 10 to 12 feeding sessions you need in a 24-hour period, and you will either need to stop swaddling at night or set an alarm to get up and feed your baby every 3 hours at night.

Once babies are past 2 or 3 weeks old, have gotten back up to their birth weight, and are more alert and awake, you can try reintroducing the swaddle at night. I mean, that's when you would prefer your baby did the majority of their sleeping anyway, right? And once that's going well and feeding is going well, feel free to try swaddling again during the day too, aiming to still get 10 to 12 feeds in a 24-hour period. Also around that 2 to 3-week mark, it can be very normal for babies to cluster feed. They may eat a lot in the evening from 5 to 8 p.m. and then take a big long nap of 5 hours after that, or maybe just 2 to 3 hours, and that is still normal. One long nap is OK for a baby who has reached their birth weight and is gaining well, as long as you can still get in enough feeding sessions. Don't become frustrated if your baby needs to take a break from swaddling. It can be fairly common in the early weeks as you and your baby are working to get feeding habits established. And don't forget to check in with your pediatrician if you are unsure that you're getting the balance of swaddling to napping to eating right—they're there to help.

Avoid Swaddling Pitfalls

- Don't use heavy blankets if you live in a warm climate. And even if you live in a cold climate or will be outdoors, make sure your baby is not overheating.

- Don't swaddle baby's legs too tightly. Swaddling the legs too tightly can lead to hip dysplasia. To avoid that, make sure your baby can stretch and move their legs if they want to. When you are judging if the swaddle is taut enough, consider that it should be taut around the chest, but loose around the legs.

- Don't swaddle your baby for longer than 3 hours at a time during the newborn period. Newborns need to eat every 2 to 3 hours; unswaddle them so they can wake and eat.

- Do not put a swaddled baby in a car seat. Crash tests only measure baby's safety in a car seat with the harness and buckles snug to the baby's body. A swaddle between the baby and the harness means the car seat cannot do its job to keep your baby safe.

- Do not put a swaddled baby down on their stomach. Stomach sleep is not recommended until babies can roll onto their bellies without assistance, and at that point you aren't swaddling anymore. Being stuck on their belly in a swaddle means your baby can't use their arms to move if they need to shift around to lift their head and breathe better.

Good-Enough-to-Eat Swaddle

Who doesn't love a good burrito wrapped up in a warm flour tortilla? Or maybe you prefer a delicious lavash wrap, rolled up tight. Oh wait, sorry; this kind of wrap won't fill your belly, but it will help you wrap your baby up nice and snug so you can have a moment of peace and enjoy that delicious burrito I just talked about! I highly recommend taking a picture of your matching burritos, both the baby and the food; just make sure you eat the correct one!

GOOD FOR: NEWBORN TO ABOUT 4 MONTHS

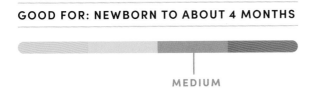

MEDIUM

1. Lay a square blanket on a flat surface turned in a diamond shape and fold the top corner down to the center of the blanket. Place the baby at the top of the blanket with the tops of her shoulders lined up parallel with the top folded edge of the blanket.

2. Hold both of the baby's arms down by her sides. Grab the blanket next to her right shoulder and pull it all the way across to the opposite shoulder, being sure to tighten up any slack or loose fabric with a gentle tug. Let the entire blanket cover her body. Roll her onto her right side and tuck the extra blanket behind her, toward the middle of her back. Lay the baby back down flat. The blanket should be wrapped around her shoulders, not her neck.

3. Grab the bottom corner and bring it up to her left shoulder. Do not pull it tight. Pass it over her left shoulder and tuck the end of the fabric behind her back, folding the fabric down so it will fit.

4. Grab the last piece of blanket by the baby's left shoulder and pull it across her body, going down toward her right hip. Then roll the baby onto her left side and wrap the blanket all the way around her back, bringing the tail of the blanket around to the front. Tuck that tail end of the blanket into the fold in the front. Voilà! You have a baby burrito!

Can't-Break-Free Swaddle

Everyone says that swaddling is great, and your little bundle does seem to enjoy it, but . . . only for the first 20 minutes of their nap. Then they wake up screaming because they have broken free from the swaddle. This one is sure to keep even the Houdini-est of babies wrapped up nice and tight!

GOOD FOR: NEWBORN TO ABOUT 4 MONTHS

MEDIUM

 1. Lay a square blanket on a flat surface turned in a diamond shape and fold the top corner down to the center of the blanket. Place the baby at the top of the blanket with the tops of his shoulders lined up parallel with the top folded edge of the blanket.

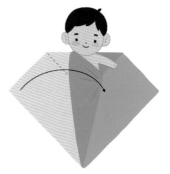

2. Hold the baby's right arm down by his side, grab the blanket by his right shoulder, and pull tight as you pass the blanket over the right shoulder and down toward his right hip. Tuck the blanket tightly under the baby's back and butt (while keeping him on his back; just tuck it under). The left arm should still be free.

3. Hold the left arm down by the baby's side and grab the bottom corner, bringing it straight up and over the baby's left shoulder and arm. Tuck the blanket tightly under his left shoulder and arm.

4. While holding the left shoulder and blanket in place and making sure his left arm stays straight, grab the remaining corner of the blanket next to the baby's left shoulder and pull the blanket taut over the baby's shoulder and down toward the baby's right hip. At his right hip, pull the blanket tight so there isn't any slack. Grab the remaining blanket "tail" and wrap it all the way around the baby, bringing it back around to the front and tucking it into the pocket of fabric that comes across the baby's front. And now, you have a snug baby who is going to stay wrapped!

Quick-and-Easy Swaddle

Your baby likes to be swaddled tightly but the crying is hitting such a high decibel level that you can't think straight, and your baby needs to be swaddled, like, yesterday, so grab a blanket and let's do this! This swaddle can be great in a pinch to help calm your baby quickly, but it has a higher Houdini rate, so it may not be best if you are trying to keep your baby swaddled and happy for long periods of time, like that wonderful afternoon nap you are hoping for later today!

GOOD FOR: NEWBORN TO AROUND 6 MONTHS

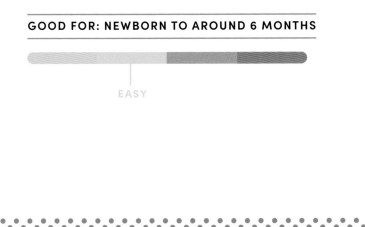

EASY

1. Lay a square blanket on a flat surface turned in a diamond shape and fold the top corner down to the center of the blanket. Place the baby at the top of the blanket with the tops of her shoulders lined up parallel with the top folded edge of the blanket.

2. Hold both of the baby's arms down by her sides. Grab the blanket by her right shoulder and pull it across the front of her body toward her left elbow and butt. Tuck the extra blanket under her back and butt.

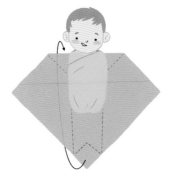

3. Grab the blanket next to her left shoulder and pull it across the front of her body toward the right shoulder and arm. Tuck the remaining fabric behind her back and butt.

4. Grab the bottom corner and bring it up and behind the baby and tuck it in the blanket that is against the back of her neck. Presto! You have a quickly wrapped baby. Now grab that baby and start walking, and you will soon have a sleeping baby!

The Let-It-Hang Swaddle

Some babies really like their arms held in, but the extra restraint that comes with pulling their legs in makes them very frustrated. And what can I say, some babies are just born with an independent streak. So instead of fighting it, embrace it and give the babies what they want!

GOOD FOR: NEWBORN TO AROUND 4 MONTHS

EASY

1. Lay a square blanket on a flat surface turned in a diamond shape and fold the top corner down to the center of the blanket. Place the baby at the top of the blanket with the tops of his shoulders lined up parallel with the top folded edge of the blanket.

2. Hold the baby's right arm down straight next to his body. Grab the blanket next to his right shoulder and pull it across the front of his body toward his left elbow and butt. Tuck the extra blanket under his back and butt, with his left arm still free.

3. Straighten his left arm down by his side, holding it in place as you grab the blanket by his left shoulder and pull it across the front of him toward his right arm and butt. Be sure to pull tight, to minimize any slack. Wrap the blanket all the way behind him and bring it back around to the front. Tuck the end of the blanket into the pocket of fabric that comes across the baby's front. Let the bottom corner just hang. You did it! You have a wrapped baby!

One Arm In, One Arm Out Swaddle

Do you have a baby who likes to be different, just seems to move to the beat of their own drum? Maybe they like the feeling of swaddling, but really miss having their hands to suck on, so they're conflicted. Or maybe (sob) you are reaching the end of your swaddling journey but your baby needs some help transitioning to a swaddle-free life. Have no fear, baby, we are here to solve all problems. How does one arm in to feel safe and secure and one arm out to suck on those yummy fingers sound? Sounds great!

GOOD FOR: NEWBORN TO AROUND 4 MONTHS

EASY

1. Lay a square blanket on a flat surface turned in a diamond shape and fold the top corner down to the center of the blanket. Place the baby at the top of the blanket with the tops of her shoulders lined up parallel with the top folded edge of the blanket.

2. Hold the baby's right arm down by her side. Grab the blanket next to her right shoulder and pull it across the front of her body toward her butt. Tuck the extra blanket under her back and butt. Make sure that the left arm does not get wrapped.

3. Lift your baby's left arm above her head, grab the blanket next to her left shoulder, and pull it across her chest toward her right arm and butt. Be sure to pull tight, to minimize any slack. Wrap the blanket all the way behind her and bring it back around to the front. Tuck the end of the blanket into the pocket of fabric that comes across the baby's front. Lower your baby's left arm back to her side. Voilà, a wrapped baby!

Swaddling from the Baby's Point of View

If you just spent the last 9 months wrapped in a warm, tight, dark cocoon and then you got thrown out into a cold, bright world, what do you think your attitude would be? Exactly. That's why I have been crying! I have not known the chilly air, separation, hunger, or a cold wet diaper on my bottom. Now that I am born, I admit it's a little cold and lonely out here just lying in a bassinet, which is usually why I cry as soon as you lay me down in it. But I have good news for both you (the new parent) and me (the new sweet adorable baby). Wrap me up and it will solve all of life's problems! Well, maybe not how to pay my college tuition, but it could give you an extra hour of sleep and less crying. When I am wrapped in a swaddle, I feel warm, safe, and secure. Who doesn't want that?

Forget the Baby, Swaddle the Parent

Parenting is hard work, and learning to be new parents together is hard work! How many times have you looked at that sweet baby, who is finally asleep after who knows how long, and thought, Wow I wish someone would swaddle me! You're right, you deserve to be swaddled. Or maybe you look at your partner, who is currently on the roller coaster of new-parenting emotions, and think, forget the baby, my spouse needs to be swaddled. Don't worry: We have all been there, and a swaddle for adults can go a long way! So if you are looking to help your partner and have a little more Zen in your house, set the baby in a swing, grab a big blanket, and start swaddling that oh-so-deserving parent who has had a hard day!

The Blowout Swaddle (sweatshirt)

You are out of the house and your baby decides to be very inconsiderate and completely poop through their diaper and clothes, and whoever packed the diaper bag (definitely not you!) forgot to pack extra clothes. Thank goodness *you* are the prepared parent and you have a sweatshirt wrapped around your waist or stashed in the car. Pull that sweatshirt off your waist and get ready to wrap that baby!

GOOD FOR: BRAND-NEW BABY UNTIL POTTY TRAINED

NOTE: Forget the blanket. Use any adult sweatshirt, preferably your partner's favorite college sweatshirt and not yours.

VERY
EASY

1. Lay the sweatshirt flat with the arms stretched out. Place the baby inside the neck of the sweatshirt, deep enough that the tops of her shoulders line up parallel with the top of the sweatshirt.

2. Pull the bottom of the sweatshirt up and fold it onto the baby's tummy.

3. Hold the fold in place; grab the right arm of the sweatshirt and cross it over the baby's body. Grab the left arm of the sweatshirt and cross it over the baby's body.

4. Tie both of the arms together, holding the bottom flap in place. Double-knot. Done! You have a clean, dry, happy baby—maybe not dressed for Sunday brunch, but you can make it home! (Warning: Don't put the baby in a sweatshirt swaddle in a car seat; the sweatshirt could interfere with the car seat, and the car seat would be unable do its job to keep your baby safe.)

Bathtime Swaddle

Whether you have a baby who loves being in the bath or one who hates it, getting out can be a pain. Either the baby is crying because they don't want to get out or because they've been begging to get out the whole time. In both cases, wrapping them up after a warm, clean bath is a surefire way to have a happy baby. Let's get started.

GOOD FOR: NEWBORN TO 12 MONTHS

NOTE: Swap the blanket for a hooded baby towel.

VERY
EASY

1. While holding the baby, place the hood on the back of her head. Then lay the baby down on a firm, flat surface.

2. Grab the left side of the towel next to the baby's shoulder and pull it across your baby's body and tuck it behind her back.

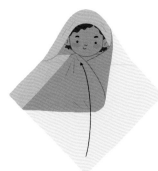

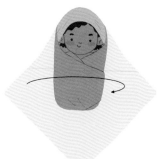

3. Grab the bottom of the towel, lift it up toward the baby's right shoulder, and tuck it behind that shoulder.

4. Grab the towel next to the baby's right shoulder and wrap it across her body, tucking it behind her back. Hold and cuddle (and, dare I say, sniff?!) your fresh, clean baby. But don't wait too long; once your baby is dry, unwrap and get that diaper back on. Don't say I didn't warn you!

Too-Tired-to-Care Swaddle

Swaddling is amazing, but these are still babies, after all, so even the best swaddlers have days where nothing is cutting it and very little sleep has been had by anyone! Sometimes you are just too tired to care. You need something quick and efficient to calm your baby, let everyone get some sleep, and then regroup. Don't sweat it: We have all been there and had those days. Some days are just about survival, and that's OK.

GOOD FOR: NEWBORN TO 99

NOTE: Maybe you should be swaddled tonight too!

VERY
EASY

1. Lay a square blanket on a flat surface turned in a square shape. Lay the baby on the blanket with arms at her sides and with the tops of her shoulders lined up parallel with the top edge of the blanket.

2. Grab the left side of the blanket, cross it over the baby, pull tight, and tuck it behind her back.

3. Grab the right side of the blanket, cross it over the baby's body, pull tight, and tuck it into the blanket behind her neck.

4. Pick up your baby and begin the shush, bounce routine. Hopefully your friends Quiet and Sleep will arrive soon.

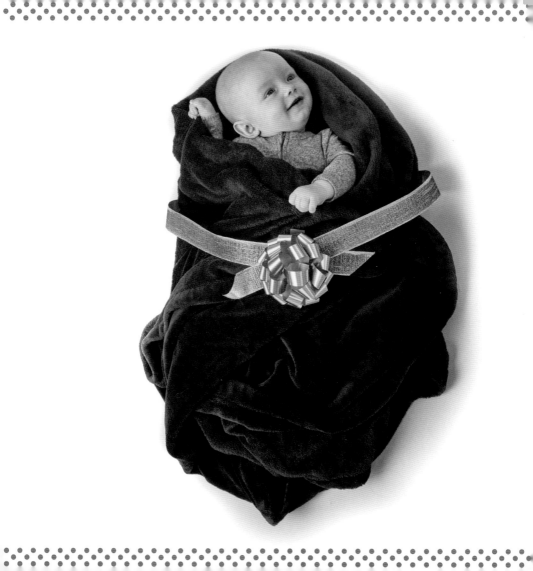

I-Got-You-a-Present Swaddle

I don't know about you, but having a baby felt like a pretty amazing gift. My husband used it as the gift that kept on giving, especially for his parents. "Happy birthday, Mom, I got you a grandchild!" "Merry Christmas, Mom, I got you a grandchild." Now that our oldest is 11, I keep reminding my husband that he cannot use our children as gifts anymore. However, those of you with sweet new babies should feel free to wrap them up and present them to those very thankful grandparents.

GOOD FOR: NEWBORN TO 6 MONTHS

NOTE: Don't forget a ribbon to decorate your freshly wrapped baby.

EASY

1. Lay a square blanket on a flat surface turned in a diamond shape and fold the top corner down to the center of the blanket. Place the baby at the top of the blanket with the tops of his shoulders lined up parallel with the top folded edge of the blanket.

2. Hold both of baby's arms down by his sides. Grab the blanket next to his right shoulder and pull it all the way across to the opposite shoulder, being sure to tighten up any slack or loose fabric with a gentle tug. Let the entire blanket cover his body. Roll the baby onto his right side and tuck the extra blanket behind, toward the middle of his back. Lay the baby back down flat. The blanket should be wrapped around his shoulders, not his neck.

3. Grab the bottom corner and bring it up to the baby's left shoulder. Turn the baby on his side again and tuck the end of the fabric behind his back, folding the fabric down so it will fit. Lay the baby back down on his back.

4. Grab the last piece of blanket next to the left shoulder and pull it across the body, going down toward the baby's right hip, and then roll the baby onto his left side and wrap the blanket all the way around the back, bringing the tail of the blanket around to the front. Tuck the end of the blanket into the pocket of fabric that comes across the baby's front.

5. Take a ribbon and place it under the baby's back; bring both sides of the ribbon up so that the ribbon is in the center of the baby. Tie a bow on his tummy.

6. Present your adorable baby gift to your loving family and then run and take a nap!

Sweet Pea Swaddle

Is it Halloween? Do you have a sweet new baby who just likes to sleep and eat? How do you dress up a baby who doesn't even want to fully extend all of their limbs yet? Have no fear, swaddling can even solve your Halloween costume problems!

GOOD FOR: NEWBORN TO 3 MONTHS

NOTE: Use a green blanket and a green beanie hat to create this adorable swaddle. For extra flair, glue a green felt leaf to the top of the beanie.

EASY

1. Lay a square green blanket on a flat surface turned in a diamond shape and fold the top corner down to the center of the blanket. Place the baby at the top of the blanket with the tops of her shoulders lined up parallel with the top folded edge of the blanket.

2. Hold both of the baby's arms down by her sides. Grab the blanket next to the right shoulder and pull it all the way across to the opposite shoulder, being sure to tighten up any slack or loose fabric with a gentle tug. Let the entire blanket cover the baby's body. Roll the baby onto her right side and tuck the extra blanket behind, toward the middle of her back. Lay the baby back down flat. The blanket should be wrapped around her shoulders, not her neck.

3. Grab the bottom corner and bring it up to her left shoulder. Turn her onto her side again and tuck the end of the fabric behind her back, folding the fabric down so it will fit. Lay her back down on her back.

4. Grab the last piece of blanket by her left shoulder and pull it across her body, going down toward her right hip. Then roll the baby onto her left side and wrap the blanket all the way around her back, bringing the tail of the blanket around to the front. Tuck the end of the blanket into the pocket of fabric that comes across the baby's front. Place a green beanie on your baby's head. Look at that adorable sweet pea. Now go get that candy!

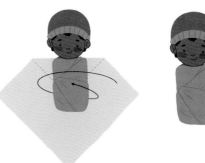

Calming Your Swaddled Baby

White Noise

It's actually not true that babies like it quiet. While they might not like hanging out at a rock concert (that's a bit much for their ears), they do like loud, soothing noises, such as the vacuum, the blow dryer, or—my favorite—the loud shushing noise straight from their parent. If you are the shushing machine, don't be afraid to get loud. You have to shush louder than your sweet little bundle can scream—I mean, sweetly cry— to create that calming effect! The volume you are going for is the noise volume of a shower: You can hear over it, but normal conversation would be hard. Your baby should have to focus on your noise and not all the outside noise.

Change of Scenery

Babies can get tired of looking at the same four walls, just like we do. Now, the prospect of getting out can seem like a lot, but you don't need a huge day out at the zoo or at the beach, just a simple walk around your block will usually do. And if the thought of hauling out the stroller is holding you back, remember that, once you know how to babywear (see page 69 to get started), you can just strap on your baby and head out!

Sway or Walk

Babies love movement, and who can blame them? They were just walked for the past 9 months straight. You don't necessarily need to get your walking shoes on, although babies do love walks. Often a walk inside your home or just moving from sitting to standing will calm a fussy baby. Still fussing after you stand? Add a little bounce or sway to your walk.

Find Your Zen

Babies cry, and that's OK. Sometimes the hardest part is to not take their crying personally. How does that saying go? They are not crying at you, they are crying with you, or something like that. Take a big deep breath and remind yourself that you are an amazing parent and this tiny bundle is lucky to have you. Say it as many times as you need to until you believe it. This baby is lucky to have you! You are both learning and getting to know each other, and that takes time. I cannot say this enough: This baby is lucky to have you!

Good Baby or Bad Baby?

Congratulations on your new baby. I'm sure your baby is the cutest one you have ever seen, and I assure you, they *are* the cutest baby ever! Now the real question is, Did you get a bad baby or a good baby? Now I admit I don't think anyone ever asked me if I had a bad baby, but that was certainly implied the millions of times (OK, maybe it just felt like a million) that I was asked if my baby was good. I admit over the years I have analyzed this question; what does "good baby" even mean? I don't think my 2-month-old who refused to ride in the car and insisted on crying any time I put him in his car seat was a bad baby. I mean, I certainly didn't think he was trying to thwart all of my attempts to get to the grocery store, but he also definitely didn't go with the flow. Did this make him a bad baby? That 2-month-old is now a very vibrant 8-year-old, who still doesn't love long car trips because he has such a strong need to move his body. So was he a bad baby at 2 months for not liking the restriction of the car seat? No, he was just a kid that needed constant movement. I promise you all babies are good. Some just have higher needs than others.

As you navigate this new world of your baby, it can get exhausting trying to understand this new language, especially if you have a higher-needs baby. I admit this higher-needs baby of mine definitely tested my patience plenty, especially since he wasn't my first (so I knew that other babies were easier), but I also knew that when I changed my perspective from "He's being difficult to make my life miserable" to "What is it that he needs help with?" I could see that he just has different needs. Our perspectives about our babies matter.

Is Crying Bad?

I remember hearing my first baby's first cry: It went straight to my core. I wanted to do everything I could to protect him, love him, and shelter him from life, but alas, that is not really life. When a baby is crying, they are communicating. Many new parents will begin to notice that their baby actually has different cries, one when they are tired, one when they are hungry, and then what I like to call the ambiguous cry. You have met all of your baby's needs—diaper change, food, warmth, being held and loved . . . and despite all these things, they are still crying. Swaddling helps calm and settle your baby, but sometimes, despite all your best efforts, crying happens. Our babies, despite being given everything they want and more, have bad days, sad days, grumpy days; it is not a reflection on you as a parent. I will just go ahead and repeat that: It is not a reflection

on you as a parent. Doing everything you can to help take care of your baby (and yourself!) through a crying fit is not the same as ignoring your baby and leaving them to cry. Being uncomfortable with our babies' crying is normal. In fact, it's good, because it calls us to action to help our babies. But their crying is also normal, and as parents this is our first opportunity to realize that our kids will have hardships in life despite all of our best efforts. Just hold them, love them, and let them show their full range of emotions. We don't have to solve all of our children's problems as parents, we just need to be there to support them while they navigate life. It's amazing that these life lessons for both our babies and us as parents start from infancy!

Babywearing

Why Babywear?

After lots of trial and error (or maybe not, if you bought this book right away!), you have learned that babies like to be held close, wrapped up, able to hear your heartbeat, and did I mention held close? Many new parents are surprised to find how much their new baby actually wants and needs to be held. Can you blame them? They have been held for the past 9 months, constantly! While swaddling can be so helpful to calm a sweet baby, keep them happy, and help them sleep, you quickly realize that life must go on. As tempting as it is to sit around and hold your sweet swaddled baby for hours (and don't get me wrong, definitely do that!), the laundry does eventually need to get done and errands do need to be run.

Babywearing has a lot of benefits for your baby. While swaddling alone can be great for many babies, lots of babies also require movement: bouncing on the birth ball, walks around the house or the neighborhood. Babywearing allows you to combine both the feeling of being wrapped and held close with movement, basically replicating that wonderful 9 months of pregnancy (definitely wonderful for your baby, despite their 3 a.m. jab to your ribs!).

In addition to creating a warm, wonderful environment that keeps your baby happy, babywearing has many benefits for you! It is fast, convenient, and oh so snuggly. If you ask me, nothing beats a warm baby wrapped to your chest! Babywearing enables you to get done what you need to get done quickly and efficiently, hands-free! You can always lug that huge car seat and stroller out of the car and make sure you find the elevator to go upstairs, or you can strap on a baby carrier, put your cute baby inside, and go wherever you want, no elevator to find, no wide doorways to fit a stroller through, and best of all, a happy, content baby while you are out and about.

Babywearing gives you the freedom to get done what you need to get done while keeping your baby happy. Win-win for all!

Babywearing Historically

I started wearing my first child right after his birth in 2010. Very often when we were out and about, I would get stopped and told how amazing my carrier was, which was often a ring sling or occasionally a wrap; after we chatted about the carrier, people would often lament that "those were not around when my kids were little." While ring slings may not have been widely popular for all that long, babywearing with just a simple piece of cloth has been around for as long as humans have been around. Strollers are a modern invention, but babies have always needed to be carried; so it is believed that babywearing was an early invention, and that makes sense. We know that women are the masters of invention (the mothers of invention? That's what I think, anyway!), so I have no doubt that when they were presented with the challenge of carrying their babies while being nomads and searching for food, they rose to the occasion. They took pieces of cloth and wrapped or tied their babies to themselves as they went out looking for food. As humans evolved and spread out to different parts of the world, different cultures created varying types of carriers that worked for their babies.

As cultures evolved, different carriers were made. Japan created the onbuhimo. A meh dai is a carrier in China. A kanga or pagne is used in Kenya. Today there are many different names, styles, types, and brands of carriers, but they all have the same goal and purpose in mind: to enable parents to safely, efficiently, and comfortably carry their baby while keeping their hands free. The multicultural knowledge of babywearing has evolved and been passed down from generation to generation. In the United States, though, once the stroller made an appearance, it quickly became the popular choice among parents.

Although the first stroller was invented in the 1700s, it wasn't until the 1950s that it started to gain popularity in the United States. By the 1950s, strollers had become affordable for the middle class and became a must-have; many parents believed that strollers fostered independence in their babies, in contrast to the lower-class mothers who were still wrapping and wearing their babies. The stroller became the symbol of the upper and middle classes, while babywearing belonged to the poor and lower classes. In the United States, carriers were known but not widely used until the early 1980s. In 1981, Mary Blois wrote a book called *Babywearing* that created a culture shift and a movement that is known today as Modern Babywearing, as Americans began to reevaluate child-rearing and their thoughts on independence. The same year that Mary wrote her book, a father in Hawaii named Rayner Garner invented the modern ring sling. His wife had been using a traditional wrap, and Rayner discovered that two rings sewn into the fabric enabled an easier and tighter fit. He marketed the product and eventually sold the rights to Dr. William Sears, who mass-produced the carriers and marketed babywearing as an option for all families, not just those that were poor. Dr. Sears is known for coining the term *attachment parenting*, describing a parenting method based on the belief that babies who are held more often gain a stronger sense of independence; the secure attachment they develop to their parents enables them to feel safe when they are ready to explore their world. But you don't have to be a proponent of any specific theory of parenting if you want to wear your baby. All you need is a desire to wear your baby, whether that's in order to make you hands-free or enable you to cuddle your baby a little more while still getting things done. Babywearing is for everyone.

ABCs of Babywearing and Safety

Our number-one concern as parents is to keep our babies safe. As convenient and wonderful as babywearing is, it can be a little daunting to make sure you are doing it correctly. The wonderful Angelique Geehan, a babywearing expert from Houston, Texas, came up with the acronym for the "ABCs" of babywearing to help you know that you're keeping your little one safe. You can not only enjoy the comfort and convenience of babywearing, but also rest assured that your baby is happy and (most importantly) safe as they are being wrapped and snuggled against your chest. And since most new parents are in a very sleep-deprived state, Geehan's quick ABC acronym makes it easy to remember the things to look out for, even in your sleepy postpartum haze.

A — Airway

Keep the baby close enough to kiss. When babywearing, the most important thing to pay attention to is your baby's airway, so you know they're breathing OK. When your baby is wrapped in a baby carrier and you bend your head down, can you easily kiss the top of their head? If not, the carrier needs to be tightened to bring the baby higher on your chest. Lift up their bottom until you can kiss the baby and then tighten any slack in the carrier so they can stay at that height without you holding them up.

Once they are close enough to kiss, check the airway. Make sure that the baby's breathing airway is open—in other words, that their chin is up off their chest. Babies who put their chin on their chest are restricting their airway. Think of your baby's airway like a straw: If you bend the straw down, it closes the straw opening. If you notice that your baby's chin is on their chest, lift their chin up and then tighten the carrier so that the body is more supported in an upright position. This can be achieved by straightening the baby's spine a little bit and tightening the carrier so they are able to be more upright. It may take time to find the right fit that supports them, but don't get discouraged; the learning curve is normal.

And, last, can you, the wearer, see baby's nose and mouth? If you can see them, and they are not obstructed, you know that the airway is open. So, remember: *Airway*—close enough to kiss, no chin on chest, and nose and mouth are visible. Look, you are a pro already! Now let's talk about the baby's position.

B — Body Positioning

Check that the carrrier supports your baby's hips, back, and core. If you babywear for any length of time, making sure baby's body is well supported, especially in these areas, is important for long-term health and growth. While the days may feel long, the years are not; babies are rapidly growing, and their bodies are changing. It's important to make sure they're in optimal positions to support their hips, back, and core muscles.

When your sweet bundle is in a carrier, their legs should be in the M position: The top points of the M are their knees, the middle bottom point of the M is their butt, and the two outside bottom points of the M are their feet. When they are in the M position, their hips are supported and allow for optimal growth. Not all carriers enable your baby's body to be in the M position. Look for carriers that support it.

C — Comfort

Take time to make sure everyone is comfortable. An uncomfortable baby won't settle in a carrier, and an uncomforable parent won't be able to babywear for as long. Babywearing has an amazing ability to keep babies happy and content, which in turn makes you a very happy and content parent. OK, maybe not always, but I find "happy baby, happy parent" to be a pretty good saying. But if the baby isn't comfortable in the carrier or you as the wearer are not comfortable, nobody is happy, and that defeats the whole point!

First, consider this: Is the baby comfortable? They may fuss when first being put into a carrier, but a quick walk around, with some pep in your step and a gentle pat on the bottom, can usually calm your sweet baby who may be having a little babywearing reluctance. (If that doesn't work, see Why Is Baby Fussing in the Carrier? on page 107 for some more babywearing tips.)

Next: Are you comfortable? Does the carrier feel tight and secure in the appropriate places? Make sure it's snug and secure, but not uncomfortable, on your shoulders, around your back, and on your waist. (For additional trouble-shooting ideas, see How to Make Your Carrier More Comfortable on page 94.) A good carrier should be as comfortable for the wearer as for the baby.

In addition to following the ABCs, here are some other things to keep in mind:

- *Babies can be worn right away, but don't rush it.* Those first few weeks should be spent mostly in bed anyway, especially for the parent who just gave birth, so don't be in a big rush to strap on that baby. Enjoy some skin-to-skin cuddles in bed. And then, when you are both in need of a little fresh air, instead of hauling out that big stroller, just strap your baby on and head out!

- *Don't give up easily.* I will always remember getting my first carrier. It was a stretchy wrap given to me by my mother-in-law at my request. When I opened that long piece of stretchy cloth, I was instantly overwhelmed and regretted picking it. Why couldn't I have gone with the one with the buckles? But I pressed on and learned how to use it, and I am so glad I did. Five babies later, it is still one of my favorite carriers, and all my babies also agreed; that carrier was able to get all of them to sleep fast!

- *Try more than one.* I rarely fit into the very first pair of jeans that I try on. It may take trying on multiple styles and sizes, and even visiting multiple stores, to discover the right pair. Finding the right baby carrier from among the many different styles and brands is no different. And just because your best friend loved one type of carrier or one brand doesn't mean it'll work for you. Find the right fit for your body.

- *One hand on baby, one hand on carrier.* When you go to use a carrier for the first time, it can be overwhelming to figure out how to put it on—let alone how to put a tiny, floppy baby inside it. As you juggle baby and carrier, it's easy to get flustered. Here's a hint: *one hand on baby, one hand on carrier.* These hands will switch back and forth, changing their role from holding the baby to adjusting the carrier. And, before you know it, they will find a natural rhythm as one hand stabilizes the baby and the other one adjusts the carrier, and then you switch, and soon you're all set.

Check Your Fit

Is your baby high enough to kiss?

Is your baby's airway clear and head not slumped over?

Are your baby's thighs supported out to their knees?

Are your baby's knees higher than their butt, and do their legs not overspread? (If the carrier extends past your baby's knees, their legs may stick out and not bend at the knee.)

Is the carrier snug, allowing your baby's back to be supported and not slump in the carrier?

Types of Carriers for Babywearing

There are several different types of carriers and, within each type, many different brands and styles. When asked which carrier is the best, I often say that is like asking me what my favorite pair of jeans is. We all fit jeans differently, so my favorite carrier may not work for you. Instead, I hope to give you some practical tips so you can find the right carrier for you, your body type, and your baby.

Types of carriers for babywearing:

- ring sling
- stretchy wrap
- woven wrap
- soft structured carrier
- meh dai

Terminology

When you are diving into a whole new world, it can be awkward trying to learn the new lingo. Here is a quick rundown of different terms within the babywearing world.

Babywearing — Using a baby carrier to hold, wrap, or buckle your baby to your body

Carrier — A device or piece of fabric used to attach your baby to your body

Rail — Typically referred to as either the top rail or the bottom rail, when discussing a wrap or a ring sling. The *top rail* is the seam of the fabric on the top of the carrier, and the *bottom rail* is the seam of the fabric on the bottom of the carrier.

Sling — Short for *ring sling*

SSC — Acronym for *soft structured carrier*

Tail — The ends of the carrier wrap or the end of the ring sling

Wearer — Anyone wearing the baby: parents, grandparents, nanny!

RING SLING

Ready to be comfortable, hands-free, and chic with that baby on your hip? Well then, familiarize yourself with the ring sling. You will be looking cute and fashionable in no time, keeping your baby happy and close to you. (See images on pages 100–106.)

DESCRIPTION: A ring sling is a single long piece of woven or supportive fabric that has one end sewn around two rings, and the opposite end of the fabric threaded through the rings, creating a loop or tube with the fabric that you place your baby in.

LOCATION: Front or hip

AGE RANGE: Newborn to 2 years old

REASONS TO LOVE IT: Easy to put on, great for quick errands or for a baby who can't decide if they want to be up or down (that baby definitely gets his indecisiveness from the other parent). And the adjustability of the fabric length means this wrap can be shared between caregivers and adjusted to each body easily.

SITUATIONS IT MAY NOT BE IDEAL FOR: The ring sling has only one shoulder of support, which is not ideal for long walks or situations where you would be holding your baby for longer than an hour, depending on your baby's age and weight. The smaller and lighter the baby, the longer you can typically wear them in a ring sling.

What to look for when buying a ring sling:

The shoulder — The area of the ring sling where the fabric is sewn around the rings is called the *shoulder*. The fabric can be sewn in many different ways—in pleats, fabric gathered together, or folded. Pleats can create a more secure fit but cap your shoulder, which can limit your mobility. A gathered shoulder allows for more movement, but it can be harder to get a more secure fit. Pleats help keep the ring sling in place on your shoulder.

Length of fabric — Ring slings typically come in small, medium, or large sizes; the main difference is in the length of the tail of the fabric. The total fabric length of the ring sling typically ranges from 53 to 72 inches [134 to 184 cm].

You typically buy the size based on your shirt size, but if you would like a longer tail that can be used to cover your baby while nursing or protect your baby from the sun, sizing up can be helpful.

Rings — Your baby's weight places a lot of strain on the rings. To sustain that, it is very important to buy a ring sling with anodized aluminum rings, and not wood rings or aluminum rings that have been welded. With welding, there is a weak point in the ring, which could break while you are wearing your baby. Wood rings can become brittle and break; they are not weight tested to hold a baby. Anodized aluminum rings are the ideal rings for a ring sling.

Type of fabric — Different types of fabric have different breathability and support. Depending on the climate where you live, different fabrics offer different benefits. Linen has good breathability for hot climates and can be very supportive, but it may take a while to soften up, and some are bothered by its wrinkled look. A woven cotton fabric is more supportive but, depending on its thickness, can be too warm for the wearer and the baby in warmer climates.

Popular ring sling brands:

Sakura Bloom — Sakura Bloom is a popular brand that comes in many colors and is well made, primarily with linen. It is very quick to wrinkle, which might bother those of you that like things clean and crisp.

WildBird — Another great choice, WildBird ring slings are primarily made with linen. They offer a variety of weaves and blends, colors, and patterns.

STRETCHY WRAP

A stretchy wrap enables you to create a warm little cocoon for your baby to snuggle into. It makes you a kangaroo with a pouch for your little joey. Read on to learn how to wrap that baby up and snuggle in. (See a stretchy wrap in use on pages 108–112.)

DESCRIPTION: A long piece of stretchy fabric, typically around 5½ yards [5 m], with hemmed edges and tapered ends

LOCATION: Front only

AGE RANGE: Newborns to 4 months or 18 pounds [8 kg] (When that weight is exceeded, the stretchy wrap may not provide enough support for your baby, making it uncomfortable for the wearer.)

REASONS TO LOVE IT: Stretchy wraps are ideal for newborns, because the carrier molds around your baby—in contrast to a more structured carrier that requires your baby to fit into the carrier. This is a great carrier for your baby's back and spine development. It enables your baby's spine to mold the way it needs to instead of forcing the spine into a structured carrier. This wrap is a "poppable carry"; once you have mastered how to put it on, you can take your baby in and out, without having to remove the carrier. This means, for example, you can put it on before you leave the house and you are ready when you arrive at the store. Just make sure that baby rides in the car seat, not in the carrier! Plus, the length of the fabric means it's possible to share this wrap between caregivers since it can be easily adjusted to a wearer's individual size.

SITUATIONS IT MAY NOT BE IDEAL FOR: It can be overwhelming to learn how to wrap and tie, especially with a brand-new baby. It has a short age range of use, as most wearers find it to be uncomfortable past 4 months or when your baby is about 18 pounds [8 kg].

What to look for when buying a stretchy wrap:

Fabric stretch — It's a personal choice, but I find that the more stretch, the easier it is to get a good fit; however, some wearers I know prefer less stretch for a more supportive carrier. A stretchy fabric can be put on very tight and then stretched to get the baby in. A less stretchy carrier can be more difficult to find the right fit right away, may need more readjusting, and can feel more restrictive.

Fabric thickness — The thicker the fabric, the warmer the carrier will be. If you live in a cold climate or your baby is born during the winter, a thick fabric is good; if you live in a warmer climate or your baby is born during the spring or summer, a thinner fabric is best.

Fabric length — Most stretchy wraps come in a standard 5 or 5.5 meters (even if you're buying in the United States), but some companies have caught on that baby-wearers come in many sizes and have started offering a shortened wrap. That way, your "tail" isn't so long when you tie off the carrier.

Popular stretchy wrap brands:

Baby K'tan — The K'tan is a hybrid of a stretchy wrap and a sling, but it fuctions similarly to a stretchy wrap. It has two premade X loops you would otherwise have to create when wrapping a stretchy wrap to your body. This makes it easier and faster to put on than wrapping one long piece of cloth. Since the K'tan is a fitted carrier, it has little ability to be adjusted; it's meant to be put on and fit right away. If you are a mom who just gave birth, it may be hard to find the right size for your changing body. Also, since the K'tan is a fitted carrier, it may be more difficult to pass back and forth between wearers of different sizes.

Boba — The Boba wrap has a lot of stretch. This can be helpful when trying to get your baby in. Remember to get the wrap tight enough from the beginning; otherwise, the baby can cause the carrier to sag.

Moby Wrap — The Moby is one of the originals. It has less stretch to it, which makes it harder to get your baby in, but once in, there's lots of support. The Moby is also a thicker fabric, so less suited for warmer climates.

Solly Baby — The Solly Baby is one of the thinnest stretchy wraps available. The thinness of the wrap typically makes it cooler and thus ideal for those who live in warmer climates.

WOVEN WRAP

Do you love the feeling of using the stretchy wrap with your baby and the closeness it provides, but have a baby that is getting too heavy to wear comfortably for long periods of time? A woven wrap is a great choice for wearers who have really enjoyed the stretchy wrap but need a more supportive option. Unlike a stretchy wrap, a woven wrap also can be used to put your baby on your back. The woven wrap can be wrapped in different ways— front, hip carry, and back carry. The possibilities of wrapping are endless if you have the time and a willing baby. (See images on pages 114–119.)

DESCRIPTION: A woven wrap is a single long piece of woven fabric (usually made on a loom) that typically has hemmed edges and tapered ends. It comes in various lengths, giving wearers many options to tie different styles for carrying on their body.

LOCATION: Front, hip, and back (See page 132 for back carrying information.)

AGE RANGE: Newborn to age 99 (A woven wrap is by far the most versatile agewise, providing the most support even for older kids, or as long as it's comfortable.)

REASONS TO LOVE IT: When used correctly, a woven wrap is a very supportive carrier that gives the wearer many options to carry their baby comfortably and safely; a lack of buckles at different points on the body may make it more comfortable for the wearer too. Also, the length of the fabric enables wearers to share the woven wrap with another person, as it is easy to adjust the wrap to a wearer's individual size.

SITUATIONS IT MAY NOT BE IDEAL FOR: A woven wrap has a steeper learning curve. It can take a while to learn how to safely wrap your baby. You cannot complete the wrapping process and then put your baby in, as you can with a stretchy wrap. You need to learn to wrap while placing your baby in the carrier. Some can also find the long piece of fabric overwhelming.

What to look for when buying a woven wrap:

Fabric type — Generally, you will find a woven wrap in a smaller boutique store or an online baby-wearing store. Various types of fabric are used; some can be hard to "break in," very stiff at first and hard to tie. Over time, and with more use, the fabric will grow softer and easier to use. Thicker fabrics will be warmer, so if you live in a warm climate, consider lighter fabrics, such as linen blends or cotton blends.

Fabric length — There are many different ways you can wrap a single wrap and different lengths of fabric to go along with different carries. A shorter-length wrap enables you to tie your baby on your hip without a big long tail hanging down; a longer wrap enables you to wrap a very supportive back carry.

Choosing the right size — To determine the right wrap for you, consider these two questions: (1) What is the size of the adult using the wrap? and (2) Which types of carries do you want to be able to do with your wrap? Buy a wrap in what is known as your "base size." This is the length that allows you to comfortably tie a Front Wrap Cross Carry (FWCC), the most common way to use a woven wrap. Wrap sizes typically are organized by numbers, such as a size 5 wrap. Keep in mind this size is based on the wrap length and is not related to the size of the wearer, although there is some correlation. Following is a chart of how wrap sizes typically correlate with your shirt size. There are also wraps that are shorter and longer than these

three base sizes, but these are the most common sizes. Keep in mind that even in the United States, most wraps are measured in meters, which is why those are the measurements offered here.

> Size 5 (XS/S) — 4.2 to 4.3 m
> Size 6 (M/L) — 4.6 to 4.9 m
> Size 7 (XL/2X) — 5.2 to 5.4 m

Popular woven wrap brands:

Didymos — Didymos, one of the original mass-produced woven baby wrap companies, creates beautifully patterned wraps. The wraps are made with a variety of fabrics, creating wraps of varied support, thickness, and texture.

Girasol — Known for their beautiful woven rainbow patterns, Girasol wraps are made from 100 percent cotton, which is very breathable for babywearing. Some weaves are thicker than others, and may be harder to learn to wrap with and can also be warmer, which may be uncomfortable for people in warmer climates.

Natibaby — Natibaby is known for the beautiful patterns and scenes that are woven into their wraps, which include 100 percent cotton, silk, hemp, and linen, providing varied thicknesses and different types of support from the wrap.

SOFT STRUCTURED CARRIER (SSC)

Does a long piece of cloth overwhelm you? Fear not. Babywearing can still be for you, thanks to the wonderful invention of soft structured carriers. Soft structured carriers (SSCs) are very popular for their ease of use as well as the support that they provide for the wearer. If you can put on a backpack, you can use a soft structured carrier. You can totally do this. Just add one wiggly baby, and it's easy as pie! (See images on pages 120–127.)

DESCRIPTION: A soft structured carrier consists of a structured-and-sewn panel of fabric, and on each side of the panel, straps that look like backpack straps. Attached to each strap is a chest buckle, creating additional support. A larger waist strap is attached to the bottom panel of the carrier; it goes around your waist and either buckles or uses Velcro to connect together. There are many brands of soft structured carriers, with a variety of features to choose from, such as facing the baby in or out, and different closures of Velcro or buckles, but the overall concept of a soft structured carrier is a panel with backpack straps and a waist strap.

LOCATION: Worn on either the front (facing in or out) or the back (See page 132 for back carrying information.)

AGE RANGE: 4 months to 18 months, on average (Some SSCs offer inserts that allow you to wear your baby in a carrier earlier than 4 months, and some SSC brands make a toddler carrier with which you can wear your baby well into their second or third year.)

REASONS TO LOVE IT: The SSC is the easiest for wearers to learn to use. It's easy to put on and simple to adjust. It provides two shoulder supports for the wearer, making it more comfortable for longer walks. It is possible to pass the carrier between wearers, with only adjustment of the buckles.

SITUATIONS IT MAY NOT BE IDEAL FOR: Some wearers have a hard time getting a good fit, as there are limitations to how much you can adjust the buckles. If you're sharing the carrier between wearers of significantly different sizes and/or body shapes, it may be hard to share because what fits well on one body shape may not be easily adjustable to another shape. Also, some find the buckles themselves uncomfortable.

What to look for when buying a soft structured carrier:

Support for baby's legs — Remember the B in the ABCs of babywearing: body positioning. It is important to find a carrier that supports your baby's butt, hips, and thighs all the way to the knees.

Facing in or out — Some soft structured carriers only face in. If you think that your baby might like to face out, find a carrier that offers both options. If it allows the baby to face out, does it still support your baby's legs in an M position?

Waist closure — Does the waist close with a buckle or Velcro? Some find the Velcro more comfortable and a better fit, but some also find that taking Velcro off with a sleeping baby or in a restaurant is too loud.

Breathability — Many carriers offer a mesh panel in the front that helps keep the carrier cool, especially if you live in a warmer climate. The panel helps prevent the baby from getting too hot.

Comfort — How wide is the front panel, and how padded are the straps? These are typically the biggest variations among carriers and may make the difference between whether or not they are comfortable for your body type. The comfort factor is best determined by trying them on.

Popular SSC brands:

Beco — Beco was one of the first soft structured carriers in which babies could face out while still sitting in an M position. They also created one of the first SSCs to enable newborns to sit in the carrier in an M position without an additional insert. They continue to offer a wide variety of carrier options for newborns through toddler-size carriers.

Ergobaby — Probably the best-known name in soft structured carriers, Ergobaby was also one of the first to offer a carrier that supported the baby in an M position. Ergobaby has continued to be innovative throughout the years, changing and adapting their various carriers to what parents need from SSCs that face in and out, as well as SSCs that safely support newborns.

Kinderpack — The Kinderpack is a lesser-known brand that is not found in big box retail stores, but that does not make the carrier inferior in any way. It is considered a very comfortable carrier and offers fun fabric patterns and also larger sizes for those who want to wear their babies into toddlerhood.

LÍLLÉbaby — The LÍLLÉbaby is one of the newer carriers on the market. It can be used for facing in or facing out and/or for back carrying—all in fun colors and patterns. LÍLLÉbaby has a very large following.

MEH DAI (also known as mei tai)

Does the wrap interest you but you find it a little intimidating? Do you like the soft structured carrier but find the buckles uncomfortable and it's hard to get the right, comfortable fit? You are not alone. Thankfully, there are still more options for you! Introducing the meh dai. The meh dai is from China and is common in East Asian cultures. It's a great hybrid between a wrap and a soft structured carrier; it can be a great carrier to explore and get comfortable with before you try wrapping. (See images on pages 128–131.)

DESCRIPTION: A meh dai is a panel of fabric with two short straps at the bottom two corners (waist straps) and two long straps at the top corners (shoulder straps). Some have additional headrests or hoods to cover your baby's head

LOCATION: Front or back (See page 132 for back carrying information.)

AGE RANGE: 6 months to 3 years (To wear a meh dai with a baby younger than 6 months, see the hack at right for a smaller baby.)

REASONS TO LOVE IT: The meh dai is a great choice for wearers who are looking for the comfort of a wrap (no buckles and lots of adjustability) but are not quite ready to learn all the wrapping techniques. The meh dai can be worn on the front or the back.

SITUATIONS IT MAY NOT BE IDEAL FOR: Because of its long straps, some wearers find it difficult to use,

especially when out of the home and outdoors in public places. I still remember trying to put on a meh dai in the pouring rain in a parking lot; it wasn't my best moment! I remember those long straps getting soaked and dirty dragging on the ground. Not everyone loves having that extra length.

FITTING A MEH DAI TO A SMALLER BABY: With a paneled carrier, the biggest obstacle to putting a smaller baby (generally, one under 6 months) into the carrier is the structured panel. The panel may be too tall and too wide to safely wear your baby. When that is the case, it is not possible to follow the ABCs of babywearing. If all you have is a meh dai and you need to make it work with your baby who is too small for the carrier, there are a couple of options to make it work safely. The meh dai panel is typically less structured than an SSC panel, enabling you to slightly alter it to better fit your younger baby.

If the panel is too tall for the baby—if she gets "lost" in the carrier and you cannot see her nose and mouth—you can fold the bottom panel of the carrier once or twice and then place it on your waist so that you are effectively shortening the panel. If the panel is too wide for your baby's legs, it can cause her to overextend her legs. To minimize the width of the panel, take a hair tie and thread it through the bottom waist straps all the way up to the bottom section of the panel, cinching it to make the panel narrow at the bottom, 3 to 4 inches [7.6 to 10.2 cm] above the waist panel. This will enable your baby to be in the meh dai in a sitting position and not have her legs overextended.

What to look for when buying a meh dai:

Width of straps — Some meh dai carriers come with thin straps; this can be helpful if you have narrow shoulders or want less fabric to adjust while putting on your carrier. Some meh dai carriers have wider shoulder straps that fan out as they get farther from the shoulder. When the wider straps are wrapped around the baby, they provide more support for the baby and ultimately the wearer.

Adjustable panel — Some meh dai manufacturers have made the panels adjustable both in the height and the width. Smaller babies need a narrow panel so their legs don't overextend; as your baby gets older, they need a wider carrier panel that can support their legs out to their knees. As your baby gets older and bigger, it can be helpful to have a taller panel that provides more back support for them.

Hood or head panel — Most meh dais offer a head support panel; some are thicker or taller than others. Some carriers also offer a hood you can use to shield your baby from the sun or if they fall asleep.

Popular mei dai brands:

Didymos — Didymos, also a manufacturer of woven wraps, has used the weave of their woven wraps to create a very supportive meh dai. The meh dais come in the same fabrics and weave patterns as the woven wraps from Didymos.

Infantino — Both accessible and affordable, Infantino's carriers have cute patterns and a great price; they're easily found in big box stores.

Like finding that perfect spot for your seat while driving, it can take time to get the right fit on a carrier. You want your carrier to be tight enough to keep your baby safe but not so tight that you feel uncomfortable. It is definitely possible to achieve both comfort and safety. Don't hesitate to work toward achieving that. If babywearing is not comfortable for you as the wearer, you will be less likely to do it long-term—and, let me tell you, the benefits of babywearing can last for a long time, so you don't want to stop prematurely. If things are uncomfortable, stick with it until you find the right fit. Your baby will thank you for it.

High enough to kiss? It can be hard to know which person to adjust first—you or baby— but lots of babywearing comfort issues for the wearer can be resolved just by making sure that baby is high enough to kiss. When the baby is high enough to kiss, they are high on your chest, creating a better center of gravity; when positioned correctly, they will not cause your body, more specifically your shoulders and back, to overcompensate for their weight pulling you forward. Keep your baby high enough to kiss and then focus on the following items to work on getting an even better fit.

Tight enough? Does it feel like your baby is hanging, or that you can't let go of your baby completely? The carrier is mostly likely not tight enough. When you reach around the carrier to the outside, do you feel loose straps or fabric? If so, pull the straps or fabric toward the area that you tighten, either the rings on a ring sling or the buckles on a soft structured carrier or the knots on a stretchy or woven wrap.

Too tight? Is the carrier digging into your shoulders, or do the straps feel too tight on your sides? While I know you are concerned that it needs to be tight for your baby to be safe, uncomfortably tight is not necessary. If the carrier feels too tight in one area, gently loosen the straps. Hold your baby with one hand while you loosen the straps with the other. Holding the baby ensures that if you loosen the strap too much, which can happen especially with buckle carriers, your baby remains safe.

Straps in the right spot? This is probably one of the most common issues I see when out and about. But it's fixable. Here are some tips to make sure the straps are in the correct place to make the carrier more comfortable.

1. Shoulders — Are the straps centered on your shoulder? Straps that are too close to your neck will put strain on your neck and won't distribute the weight throughout your shoulders.

2. Waist strap — If your carrier has a waist strap, is it sitting too high, or is it too low? If the strap seems to be pushing on your hip bones, loosen it and lift it up higher on your waist off your hip bones. If the carrier feels too tight or too high on your waist, loosen it and lower it.

3. Does your carrier have a strap or piece of wrap fabric that goes across the back? Any back straps should be in the center of the back between your shoulder blades. If it is a buckle strap for a soft structured carrier, make sure the strap is in the center of your back, not resting on your neck or too close to your neck; this puts too much strain on your neck. When the straps and passes are spread across the center of the back, they distribute the weight of your baby across your back and not your neck. If part of the wrap fabric goes across your back, make sure that the fabric is not twisted or bunched up. Spread the fabric across your back; this will help distribute the weight instead of having it pull on one area of your back.

Face In or Face Out

There are several ways to wear your baby: front facing in, front facing out, on your hip, or on your back. (See page 104 for more on hip carrying and page 132 for more on back carrying.) Front facing in is known as the "heart-to-heart" position and can be done right away after birth. Front facing out means their back is against your chest; you should wait to carry front facing out until your baby is 3 to 4 months and has good head control. Babywearing of any kind should be done with the right carrier for your baby's size and while following the ABCs (see page 72). The front facing out position became popular in the '90s, when a carrier came on the market that allowed for it. And as with anything related to babies, there are some guidelines you should follow to ensure your baby is safe. Let's talk about those.

The first thing you want to pay attention to is selecting a carrier that supports the baby in the M position when they're facing out (see page 74 for a visual). This position supports the baby's thighs, which ensures the baby's hips are being supported. Carriers that don't support the thighs could aggravate the condition of hip dysplasia, which some babies are predisposed to. According to the International Hip Dysplasia Institute, a carrier that supports babies' thighs from knee to hip and that keeps the thigh pulled up to at least hip level is important for proper hip development.

The second guideline to be aware of is that when babies face out, they can get overstimulated. When a baby faces in, they are able to look out to the left or right; however, if they are overstimulated by their environment (such as a large gathering or busy place), they are able to turn in toward their parent for safety and security and to block out some of the sensations. A baby facing out has no place to turn, and if you're not aware of the possibility of overstimulation, it's possible to think your baby is just fussy and try to soothe them by rocking or bouncing, rather than turning them in. I witnessed this once on a Halloween night as my kids trick-or-treated on a very busy street. While the baby may have started the night really enjoying the opportunity to look out and see all that was going on, he had clearly hit a point that he needed a break, but he had nowhere to turn. When choosing to face out, it is best to keep it to 30 minutes or less and pay attention to your baby's cues. If your baby starts to get fussy, especially if you are in a particularly overwhelming environment, stop and switch them around. You can put the baby on your hip or give them the opportunity to face completely in, take a break, and maybe even take a nap.

The third guideline to be aware of is that babies should not sleep in the forward-facing position. When they fall asleep, their heads fall forward, which can block their airways. There is that A word again (see page 73)—when a baby is facing out and asleep, their airway is not clear.

Remember: You are the expert on your baby. Listen to your baby and trust your intuition. If facing out doesn't feel good for either of you, don't do it. If your baby loves it and you do as well, strap them on facing out and go exploring together.

How to Wear a Ring Sling on Your Front: **Heart-to-Heart Hold**

A ring sling is put on like you'd wear a cross-body bag. It can be worn on either the right shoulder or the left. Some prefer to wear it on the shoulder of their dominant hand, but it can be worn on whichever shoulder is the most comfortable for you. For this tutorial, we will use the right shoulder. Preadjusting and tightening the ring sling before putting your baby in it makes it easier to get a tight fit with your baby and improves the ability to get a more comfortable fit for you, the wearer. The less adjusting after the baby is in the carrier, the better, for both you and your baby.

1. Place your hand over the rings, with the tail of the sling to the right. Put your left hand through the loop of the sling. Pull the sling up over your left shoulder and head. Rest the rings right below your right shoulder, making sure the tail is hanging down toward the floor. (If the tail is hanging over your shoulder and down your back, the ring sling is facing the wrong way.)

2. Bend your left arm at the elbow and slide your elbow and left arm down into the sling. Your right arm will be inside the carrier, with your hand sticking out of the top of the carrier. Grab the top rail of the ring sling by the rings and pull down, allowing the sling to become snug around your arm. (Do not grab the entire tail of the ring sling all at once; treat the tail like it is made up of several strands of fabric, and pull through one strand at a time.) Then grab the bottom rail of fabric and pull it down, allowing the bottom of the sling to become tight around your elbow and arm. This trick works best for babies less than 3 months of age. As your baby gets older, you will have developed a better feeling for how loose the carrier needs to be in order to slide your baby in. A tighter fit is generally easier to adjust than a too-loose fit. If it is too tight, gently lift up on the bottom ring, releasing more fabric for your baby to fit in the sling.

3. Pick up your baby and lay her against your left shoulder as if burping her. Use your right hand to support your baby on the back and butt. Move your left hand under the bottom fabric of the ring sling, bringing your hand out of the top so you can grab your baby's legs and gently guide your baby down into the ring sling, into the pouch created between the two edges of fabric. Always keep one hand on the baby and one hand adjusting the ring sling, rotating hands as needed.

4. With your baby in the ring sling, encourage the baby to sit in an M position, with her butt (the bottom middle point of the M) sitting deeply in the sling fabric and her legs and feet coming out of the sling.

5. To tighten the ring sling, grab the top rail and pull down, making the sling taut around your baby's back. Next, grab the bottom rail of fabric and pull down, making the bottom rail taut around and under the baby's butt. Your baby should feel comfortable and secure; if your baby does not seem secure, continue to tighten the rails until your baby's position feels secure. The bottom rail of the fabric should be taut around the baby's butt and also taut against your body.

6. Comfort: Check that the rings are in a comfortable position below your right shoulder, typically resting right below your collarbone. Next, reach behind your back and make sure the fabric wrapping across your back is spread out and not bunched up. This will help distribute the weight of your baby evenly across your back. Voilà, you are now comfortably wearing your baby!

How to Wear a Ring Sling on Your Hip: Ring Sling Hip Carry

As your baby gets older, they may be less interested in snuggling and more interested in seeing the world. Can you blame them? As they get older, they gain more neck and body control and, around 4 to 6 months, naturally start transitioning from a heart-to-heart hold toward being held on your hip. Anyone who has held their baby on their hip in their arms for a long period of time knows how exhausting it can be. Some people are hesitant to wear their baby on their hip, thinking it will be just as tiring, but thankfully it's not. With a carrier supporting your baby, you are able to mainly use your back muscles to support your baby. This can be a game changer; it allows you to wear your baby more comfortably and for longer periods of time while they have the freedom to look out at the world. In fact, the hip carry is perfect for world exploration. Note: For the tutorial that follows, we are focused on the right side; if you prefer the left, just reverse all the instructions.

1. Place your hand over the rings, with the tail of the sling to the right. Put your left hand through the loop of the sling. Pull the sling up and over your shoulder and head. Rest the rings directly below your right shoulder, making sure the tail is hanging down toward the floor. Adjust the ring sling by tightening the top and bottom rails individually so the sling is not too loose. You should be able to slide a small pumpkin into the pouch.

2. Pick your baby up and lay her against your left shoulder as if burping her. Use your left hand to support your baby on the back and butt. Move your right hand under the bottom fabric of the ring sling, bringing your hand out of the top of the ring sling so you can grab your baby's legs and gently guide your baby down into the sling, into the pouch created between the two edges of fabric. Always keep one hand on the baby and one hand adjusting the ring sling, rotating hands as needed.

3. Lower your baby down until she sits in the hammock of the fabric. Tighten the top and bottom rails of the carrier. Most babies on the hip will prefer to have their arms out. Make sure the top rail is at your baby's mid-back.

4. Your baby should feel secure and be high enough to kiss. If she is not high enough, lift her bottom until you can kiss the top of her head and then tighten the top and bottom rails of the sling so that she will stay there. Now enjoy exploring the world with your baby.

Time — Take your time putting on the carrier; don't rush it. Sometimes you're halfway through putting the carrier on, and your baby is really upset from all the fidgeting. Take a break from putting the rest of the carrier on; walk and bounce a little until your baby settles, and then try again. If you give yourself time to get calm again, this will help your baby settle.

Walk — Babies often don't like to be stationary in a carrier, especially when you first put them in. Once they have drifted off into a peaceful sleep, you can sit down and catch up on your latest book or video game. Unless you have a busier baby—in which case you may need to keep moving the whole time. Hey, at least your house will be extra clean from all of the vacuuming you can do. Or you might get to finish a whole audiobook while you stroll around the neighborhood! Parenting is all about finding the silver lining.

Bounce — Sometimes walking isn't enough. Your kid is hoping to be the next *Dancing with the Stars* contestant and they are ready to practice, now. A little bounce while walking keeps them happy. Now this doesn't mean you need to practice the tango, but a little bounce will definitely help. As you walk, bend your knees just a little, so that baby feels more vigorous movement. While babywearing is meant to be a hands-free event, when bouncing, it may feel necessary to hold on to your baby to make them more supported (especially if you have a little one that needs neck support). Listen to that instinct and hold your baby as you gently bounce them.

Feed — If mom is breastfeeding and she is doing the wearing, the baby can smell that milk. The baby thought he had had enough but, after smelling mom, decided he had a little extra room! I think we can all relate. Don't judge. Your baby is a growing human; feed him. Try babywearing a little later, when his tummy is full again and maybe sleep is on the horizon.

How to Wear a Stretchy Wrap: Heart-to-Heart Hold

There are various ways a baby can be worn in a stretchy wrap, but I find the ideal position for a stretchy wrap is facing in, heart-to-heart. In this position, your baby is able to meet all the safety markers—high enough to kiss, with their nose and mouth visible.

1. Find the middle marker of the wrap (there's a tag). Place and hold the marker in the center of your chest, with each side of the wrap lying on the ground to the right and left.

2. While holding the middle marker with your left hand, grab the right side of the wrap and wrap it around your back; pull it up over your left shoulder, and let it hang over your shoulder and down the left front of your body. (While wrapping it around your body, take care that the wrap does not become twisted. To minimize twisting the fabric, hold the wrap on the top rail only, rather than grabbing the entire wrap in a bunch.)

3. Next, grasp the left side of the fabric, again holding only the top rail, and wrap it around your waist, behind your back, and up over your right shoulder, letting the wrap lie over your right shoulder and hang down the right side of your body. You should now have what looks like a cummerbund around your waist, and two pieces of fabric that have made an X on your back and hang over each shoulder.

4. Grab both tails of the wrap and cross the right piece over the left piece, making an X in the front, then tuck both pieces of the wrap underneath the cummerbund, and pull them all the way through, keeping the X intact, pulling the passes of the wrap tight against your body. Tightness is the key; you do not need to leave any space for your baby, as the material will stretch. While keeping the fabric in an X, wrap both pieces of fabric around your back, cross them again behind your back, and then bring the ends forward and tie in a double knot.

5. There is now an X of fabric on your chest; the left panel of the X is closest to your body, while the right panel is lying over the left panel. Pick up your baby, putting her on the right shoulder (opposite the side of the fabric that is closest to your body) as if you are going to burp her. Keep one hand firm on your baby's back and butt, supporting her. Bring your left hand under the left pass and go up toward your baby on the right. Grab your baby's legs and guide them down into the left pass, allowing them to straddle the left pass, one leg to the left and one leg to the right. Then spread the fabric of the pass across baby's butt all the way to behind the knees.

6. Hold your baby with your left hand. Grasp the right pass and pull it over your baby, allowing your baby to straddle the right pass as well, with the pass spread all the way across the butt to your baby's knees.

7. Next, reach down and grab the cummerbund that you created in the beginning and pull it up over your baby's legs and butt, up to her mid-back. Her legs can be covered or not. Make sure the baby is close enough to kiss and feels securly tied in, then enjoy those sweet baby snuggles.

Optional: If your baby is sleeping or wants to rest her head, lay her head on your chest and cover the back of her head with either the left or right pass, providing head and neck support for your baby while she snuggles and sleeps. If your baby does not have proper head control and does not want to lay her head down, you will need to keep your hand close to her head to provide the necessary head support as she explores her surroundings.

How to Find the Right Carrier for You

The best way to find the right carrier for you is to try them on. It may not always be possible to go to a store and try on all the carriers. When online shopping, here's how to narrow it down to a couple that might work for you.

1. *When you read about each carrier, which one appeals to you?* Some people right away think, *Buckles, that's what I want.* Others like the idea of a wrapping carrier. I heard one dad say he was a master at tying knots, so he knew he wanted to wrap.

2. *Where do you think you will be wearing your carrier the most?* If you will be at home, you might have the time to put on a wrap. Or if you'll be running a lot of errands in the car, a ring sling or soft structured carrier may be best for putting on quickly in a parking lot.

3. *What features do you want?* Consider if you will eventually want to put your baby on your back or be able to face them forward on your chest. If so, a soft structured carrier is probably the right carrier for you.

4. *What is your body type?* Wraps and meh dais enable a more individual fit and are the most adjustable. A soft structured carrier with buckles is limited in the areas of tightening and finding the right fit. Read the size adjustment dimensions on carriers to find the one that best fits your body type.

5. *Which carrier do you like the most aesthetically?* Consider which one you can see yourself wearing. With babywearing, most people will see your carrier more than the shirt you are wearing. Even if the carrier you choose seems practical and is at the right price point, if you don't like it or think it's cute, you may not want to put it on every day. So, pick one that is practical for your style!

6. *Each type of carrier has different benefits and features.* Read each section about the different baby carriers and narrow it down to which features might work for you and your baby. Then you can select a few carriers to try out.

How to Wear a Woven Wrap:
Front Wrap Cross Carry (FWCC)

A woven wrap is very versatile, with many different ways you can wear it and tie it. The Front Wrap Cross Carry is a very supportive carry for both baby and wearer. It enables your baby to be heart-to-heart with the wearer and is ideal if you will be wearing your baby for a long period of time (more than an hour) or if you anticipate your baby will be falling asleep. This carry is very supportive and comfortable for wearing your baby.

1. Find the middle marker of the wrap. Place and hold the marker in the center of your chest, with each side of the wrap lying on the ground to the right and left.

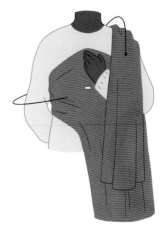

2. While holding the middle marker with your left hand, grasp the right side of the wrap, wrap it around your back, and pull it up over your left shoulder; let it hang over your shoulder and down the left front of your body. (While wrapping the wrap around your body, take care that the cloth does not become twisted. To minimize twisting the fabric, hold the wrap only on the top rail, rather than grabbing the entire wrap in a bunch.)

3. Next, grasp the left side of the fabric, holding only the top rail, and wrap it around your waist, behind your back, and up over your right shoulder, letting the wrap lie over your right shoulder and hang down the right side of your body. You should now have what looks like a cummerbund around your waist, and two pieces of fabric that have made an X on your back and hang over each shoulder. Double-check that the passes on your back are not twisted or bunched up. The more spread out the passes are, the more support the wrap provides and the fewer pressure points are created. Pull the right top and bottom rails and the left top and bottom rails of the wrap to tighten your cummerbund so that there is just enough room to slide your hand underneath the cummerbund. The more fitted the wrap feels before you place your baby in it, the easier it will be to get a good fit with your baby.

4. Pick up your baby and place her over your right shoulder. Hold her back with your right hand. Slide your left hand up and under the front panel that you have made, up toward your baby's legs and butt. Grab your baby's butt and help guide her body down into the panel. Allow her legs to come out the bottom of the panel and then make a hammock with the cummerbund panel that her butt can sit in. The bottom of the panel should come up between you and your baby, up to the top of her diaper, to create a deep seat for her to sit in. If the panel does not want to come up, lean forward, keeping one hand securely on her back, to create a space between you and the baby, and then reach down between the two of you and pull up on the bottom rail toward her belly to create a deeper seat. For a newborn, the cummerbund panel should come up to your baby's neck. For babies with more head control, the panel can come up to mid-back so your baby can hold her arms out.

5. While holding your baby securely with your hand on her back, grab the right pass and pull down on the top rail, the middle rail, and the bottom rail. It is helpful to think of a woven wrap as strands of fabric instead of one piece of fabric; you need to tighten each strand (or rail). As you tighten each rail on the right pass, you will see that the cummerbund begins to tighten, holding your baby in more securely. When the right pass feels safe and secure, bunch it up and hold it tight with your right hand; then place your right hand against baby's back (while also holding the pass) for extra support as you begin to tighten the left pass.

6. While holding the right pass, begin tightening each rail of the left pass by pulling down on each rail. When both passes feel secure, grab them both and first lift them up toward the sky and then pull them down. This will ensure that the wrap is tight and secure. (Your wrap should be secure enough at this point that you can let go of your baby and just hold the passes. If it does not feel secure, keep tightening each rail until it feels secure.)

7. Grab both passes and cross them over each other, making an X underneath baby's bottom. Wrap both passes behind your back and tie off with a knot. Enjoy a hands-free moment with your baby.

How to Wear a Soft Structured Carrier: Facing In

All soft structured carriers allow for the baby to face inward in a heart-to-heart hold. This position is comfortable for both the wearer and the baby. It is also the ideal position for a baby who is ready to take a nap. It enables your baby to rest their head on your chest. Who doesn't love a good nap snuggle from their baby?

1. Place the waist strap against your waist, with the panel hanging down and the inside of the panel facing out (so when you put on the arm straps, the inside is against your body). Buckle (or Velcro) the waist strap behind your back. Tighten the buckle, so it feels comfortable and taut around your waist.

2. Pick up your baby and hold her against your stomach facing you, with her sitting right on top of the waist strap and her legs wrapped on each side of your body.

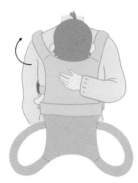

3. Hold your baby's back with your left hand. Grasp the panel with your right hand and lift it up over your baby's back. With your hand on the outside of the carrier, hold your baby and carrier with your right hand, pull your left hand out from under the panel, and place your left hand through the left strap and up onto your shoulder.

4. Switch hands. Now support your baby with your left hand on the outside of the carrier, holding her back. Grab the right strap with your right arm and put it on over your shoulder.

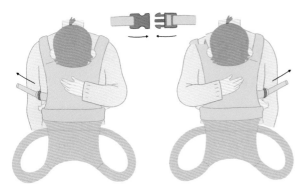

5. Now you need to buckle the clip that is on your back. You have a couple of options. Ask a very nice nearby adult to buckle and tighten it for you. Or, if you are alone, loosen the sides of the shoulder straps so they are very loose, make sure your baby is safely in the middle of the center panel, and then reach both hands behind your neck and buckle the chest clip. Then grab your baby with your left hand, lifting her bottom, and tighten the right shoulder strap with your right hand. Then switch; lift your baby's bottom with your right hand and tighten the strap on the left shoulder. Remember, your baby should be high enough to kiss and feel secure. The chest clip should ideally be in the middle of your back between your shoulder blades. If your baby is slightly off center, you can reach inside the panel of the carrier and adjust her butt so she is sitting centered in the panel.

6. Make any additional tightening adjustments that you need and then enjoy the hands-free snuggles with your baby.

How to Wear a Soft Structured Carrier: Facing Out

Some carriers offer the option for a baby to face out. This option is great for a curious baby who has good head control. When you are ready to face your baby out, first adjust the panel on your soft structured carrier to make sure it is in the face-out position. This adjustment looks different on each carrier.

1. Place the waist strap against your waist, with the panel hanging down and the inside of the panel facing out (so when you put on the arm straps, the inside is against your body). Buckle (or Velcro) the waist strap behind your back. Tighten the buckle, so it feels comfortable and taut around your waist.

2. Pick up your baby, face him out, and sit his butt on the top on the waist panel that is up against your waist. Holding your baby with one hand, use the other hand to pick up the panel that is lying against your legs.

3. Hold the panel against your baby's belly, while also using that hand now to support your baby. Use your other hand to put the carrier on like a backward backpack. Pull one strap up and over your shoulder, switch hands supporting the baby, and put the other strap over your shoulder.

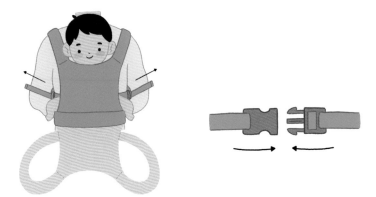

4. Check to make sure your baby is centered on your body, not leaning too far to the left or right. Adjust the straps under your arms to make sure the carrier is secure on your body. Once your baby feels centered and secure, either reach both hands behind your head and buckle the chest clip or ask a fine person near you to buckle the clip and make sure it is in between your shoulder blades for optimal comfort. Enjoy the world with your baby. If your baby becomes overwhelmed or sleepy, just stop and turn him inward.

How to Wear a Meh Dai:
Heart-to-Heart Hold

A meh dai is typically worn with your baby facing in, in a heart-to-heart position. Many meh dai carriers can be worn inside out, as there is a pattern on both sides of the carrier. So be sure and pick the side that you want facing out before you get started.

1. Place the bottom waist panel against your waist, with the body panel hanging down and the inside of the panel facing out (so when you put on the arm straps, the inside is against your body). Tie the waist straps behind your back with a double knot.

2. Pick up your baby and hold her heart-to-heart, with her butt against the top of the waist panel. Use your right hand to hold your baby's back while you lift the panel up and over her back with your left hand. Place one strap over each of your shoulders.

3. Place your left hand on the baby's back. Bring your right hand out from underneath the panel; reach around your back, and grab the strap that is hanging over your left shoulder. Bring the strap around to your front, and hold the strap and the baby's back. Use your left hand to reach around your back and grab the strap that is hanging over your right shoulder and bring it around your back to the front of your waist. Pull both straps to get out any slack, and make the panel tight against your body.

4. With both straps in the front, cross them over each other underneath your baby's bottom and then pull them back toward your back, going under your baby's legs and tying in a double knot on your back. Check and make sure your baby is snug and secure. Enjoy the freedom of hands-free!

Back Carrying

That sweet bundle has now become a slightly bigger bundle, and while you have enjoyed holding them on your front, their cute chubby arms and legs are starting to get in the way a little bit. *When I saw that mom at the park the other day, she had her baby on her back, and that looked so comfortable and freeing. Um, I mean, so good for the baby!* But is that safe for the baby? The answer is yes! Let's talk more about how to do it safely.

Babies can be put on your back around 6 months, when they have learned to sit unassisted, when they can hold themselves up and support their airway. Babies who are older than 6 months are also better able to help support themselves and hold on while you put them on your back. (Please note: Many other cultures, and experienced babywearers, wear their babies much earlier on their backs. No need to judge another parent at the park and their safe wrapping skills when they are back-carrying a 2-month-old.)

It can definitely be a little intimidating to put your baby on your back. But, as the saying goes, necessity is the mother of invention. For me, it was necessary to put my baby on my back. He simply became too big for me to get anything done with him on my front, and setting him down was still not OK with him; so, moving to the back was the next best option. Back carrying is an advanced carry and takes some time to learn, but don't be discouraged. Just remember when you thought having a baby, let alone swaddling and babywearing, was advanced—and now all that is old hat. If your baby is 6 months and you have been babywearing for several months, you are a pro now; you are ready for this next level, and so is your baby. Back carrying is best learned in person with an experienced wearer or by watching videos. To help back carrying be a safe and positive experience for you, I have chosen *not* to include instructions for different back carries. Instead, I encourage you to seek out a local babywearing group or friend to help you, or to watch the many back-carrying videos that will enable you to safely and comfortably wear your baby on your back.

Although I am not going to teach back wearing in this book, I will provide information about what carriers are best for back carrying, and also some extra tricks, tips, and resources to help you have a more positive back-carrying experience if you decide to start exploring and try it. Think of this as an addendum to watching videos or any in-person learning you do on back carrying.

Ring Sling — A ring sling is not an ideal carrier for back carrying. If your baby is 6 months or older, sitting on your hip in the ring sling and beginning to grab everything, and you need to stir a hot pot or cut something with a knife, your baby can be scooted to your back for a moment (be sure to tighten the ring sling after you move your baby to your back so they are secure). But your baby should be brought back to your hip in 5 minutes or less since this isn't as secure as other wraps for back carrying.

Stretchy Wrap — It is not safe to wear a baby on your back in a stretchy wrap. Your baby could lean back in the wrap, and the elastic in the wrap would not support them, so they could fall.

Woven Wrap — This carrier is ideal if you have been wrapping your baby on the front for a couple of months and feel very comfortable with wrapping your baby. While the wrap has the steepest learning curve, it can be the most comfortable carrier for the wearer and the baby, as there are no buckles. It is also typically the most supportive carrier for the wearer, enabling the wearer to wear their baby well into toddlerhood.

Soft Structured Carrier — The soft structured carrier is typically the easiest to learn to back-carry with. It allows you to put the carrier on first, then put your child on your back, and then pull the carrier on over your baby. The buckles make it also the fastest carrier to put on. For long periods of back wearing and the older a child gets, it can be less supportive than other carriers (e.g., a woven wrap); however, for many wearers, the ease of use outweighs the lack of support it provides for older babies.

Meh Dai — The meh dai is great for back carrying. It has the ease of use of a soft structured carrier but also provides the support and customization of a woven wrap. The built-in panel makes it easier to get on than the woven wrap; but the long tails to tie off make it a little more difficult than a soft structured carrier with buckles.

Tips When Learning to Back-Carry
You will not always need these tips, and eventually back carrying will feel as easy as front carrying,

but when you are getting started, these tips can help ease the learning curve.

- *Do it over the bed.* The best place to start practicing putting your baby on your back is standing next to your bed. Then you know that your baby has a safe place to land if they do fall while you are putting them on your back.

- *Do it in front of a mirror.* Put a floor-length mirror next to your bed while you practice; it can help you to see what you are doing.

- *Do it with a spotter.* It is ideal to have someone to help you and keep an eye on your baby as you practice putting your baby on your back.

- *Do it when the baby is ready.* This means both when your baby is old enough and when your baby is fed, not tired, and happy to try something new.

- *Do it when you are ready.* Back carrying is a new skill, and new skills take time. I guarantee you that the mom who you saw throw a baby on her back at the park or on that YouTube video you watched did not look like that the first time she tried.

Top 6 Survival Tips for New Parents

1. *Do what works for you and leave the rest.* I remember when I was pregnant for the first time, there was so much advice! But I also remember that for so many people, it wasn't advice; they believed that what they were telling me was the *only* way to raise my baby. Like anyone, I have found many things that work for me and my family, and I couldn't imagine doing it any other way. But after years of helping so many different families, I am constantly reminded that there is no one-size-fits-all approach to raising a baby.

2. *Family needs and lifestyles are all different.* So just because your friend insists that you must buy and use a swing for your baby doesn't mean that you really have to. I've had babies who love the swing and we couldn't live without it—and others that refused to stay in it for 5 minutes. I know families who insist on a night nurse, and that they couldn't have done it without them. My husband and I agreed that while nights were

hard, they weren't as bad as people said, and we loved doing it on our own. Different ways just work differently for different families. When a mom calls me because a friend or her mother has told her what she is doing is wrong, I ask, "Is it working for your family?" If she says yes, then I remind her to repeat the phrase, "This is what works best for our family." No one can disagree with that statement.

3. *Babies change—a lot!* When my baby was little, it seemed like the number-one question I got was, "What is his sleep schedule?" Everyone seemed so fascinated with his routine. I was getting asked this question as early as a month old, and just as soon as I would say something, he would decide to change. In the beginning, this question really got to me and made me feel like a failure, because I couldn't seem to get a handle on his schedule. He would shorten a nap, moving up the time of the next one, or he would stay up longer, extending the time till the

next nap. Just as soon as I felt like we had it, a nap at 9, a nap at 1, and bedtime at 8, he would mix it up. Until finally someone clued me in: Babies change—a lot! What was happening with my little boy was totally normal, and totally fine for us. He was just growing and changing. It's not you; it's definitely your baby!

4. *Babywear!* Most babies love to be held, and it's wonderful to hold them. But life has to go on, and you cannot hold them all day long . . . though, thankfully, with babywearing you can. Find the right carrier, strap your baby on, and keep both of you happy. Your baby is held and snuggled and you are hands-free to continue to get stuff done.

5. *Think of your baby as human.* When everyone was asking me what my baby's schedule was, I often felt like they expected my baby to behave like a robot on a perfect schedule. And it would have been very nice for my baby to nap and wake up at the same time, eat the same foods and the same amount every day—at least in theory. But the fact is, our babies are humans like us. They have days when they need more food or not quite as much as yesterday, days where they need more or less sleep. I'm not sure why they refuse to nap on the day that you have something very pressing to do during nap time, but that's how babies are; just as you

have tired days, lazy days, and active days, so does your baby. Despite all the crying, peeing, and pooping, they are more like you than you think!

6. *Ask for help.* I admit this piece of advice was hard for me. My type A personality liked to do things all by myself. In my life before kids and before professionally helping others with their babies, I was an executive assistant. I was used to helping others, but not allowing others to help me. I soon realized that my "do it myself" attitude was going to need a little adjustment. With anything, the goal is a happy balance. I needed to learn to do some things on my own to raise my confidence in taking care of my baby, and I'm grateful to those who gave me the space to do that. But also, when I needed support, I had a village that was willing to help. Find your village, find those who align with your baby-raising beliefs, and don't hesitate to ask for help, whether it is for someone to hold your baby while you shower, commiserate with that this is hard, or celebrate how amazing this journey is. Someone who can relate to the lows, celebrate the highs, and not judge your choices—only offer advice and change a blowout diaper like it's no big deal. This parenting journey has highs and lows. Surround yourself with people who not only celebrate it all but also help with it all.

Additional Babywearing Education:

Baby Wearing | Ask Dr. Sears — A trusted pediatrician and resource for all things parenting, Dr. Sears is also a certified babywearer, and his website has lots of babywearing advice and information.

www.askdrsears.com/topics/
health-concerns/fussy-baby/
baby-wearing/

Wrap Your Baby — This baby wrap brand not only sells woven wraps but also has lots of resources for babywearing generally and can help you find local baby-wearing groups.

www.wrapyourbaby.com

More about Co-sleeping:

Safe Infant Sleep by James J. McKenna, PhD (2020) — This book provides everything families need to know about safely sharing a bed with their baby, along with research on the benefits of co-sleeping for parents and babies.

Sweet Sleep by La Leche League International (2014) — A guide for making safe decisions on where and how your family sleeps, including evidence-based information about co-sleeping and how it relates to sleep.

Back-Carrying Resources:

BabywearingFaith — Faith is a babywearing educator whose YouTube channel includes lots of different types of carriers, as well as lots of ways to use each carrier.

www.youtube.com/user/BabywearingFaith/videos

Wrap Your Baby — This is a wonderful website that offers lots of information on wrapping your baby with a woven wrap; they also sell woven wraps.

www.wrapyourbaby.com

Wrapping Rachel — Rachel is a certified babywearing consultant who has dozens of videos that help wearers learn different ways to safely and comfortably wear their baby.

www.wrappingrachel.com

Recommended Brands:

While I mention many brands of baby carriers within the book, below are some of my personal favorites.

Beco — www.becobabycarrier.com

Didymos — www.didymos.com

Ergobaby — www.ergobaby.com

Kinderpack — www.mykinderpack.com

Sakura Bloom — www.sakurabloom.com

Solly Baby — www.sollybaby.com

WildBird — www.wildbird.co

Wrap Your Baby — www.wrapyourbaby.com

a

attachment parenting, 72

b

babies. *See also* babywearing; sleeping; swaddling

calming, 64–65

crying, 64–65, 67

feeding, 19–20, 107

"good" vs. "bad," 66

as individual personalities, 11, 138

skin-to-skin cuddling with, 17, 19

weight gain by, 20

Baby K'tan, 83

babywearing. *See also* back carrying; carriers

ABCs of, 72–75

benefits of, 10, 69–70, 138

definition of, 78

facing in vs. facing out, 96–97

history of, 70–72

safety and, 72–74

tips for, 75–77

back carrying, 132–36

Back to Sleep campaign, 15

Bathtime Swaddle, 49–51

Beco, 89–90

blankets, 16, 21

Blois, Mary, 71

The Blowout Swaddle, 45–47

Boba, 83

bottom rail, 78

c

Can't-Break-Free Swaddle, 27–29

carriers. *See also* meh dais; ring slings; SSCs; wraps, stretchy; wraps, woven

choosing, 76, 97, 113

comfort and, 75, 94–95

definition of, 78

fussing babies and, 107

history of, 70–71

types of, 78

car seats, 21

co-sleeping, 16

crying, 64–65, 67

d

Didymos, 86, 93

e

Ergobaby, 90

f

feeding, 19–20, 107

Front Wrap Cross Carry (FWCC), 86, 114–19

g

Garner, Rayner, 72

Geehan, Angelique, 72

Girasol, 87

Good-Enough-to Eat Swaddle, 23–25

h

Heart-to-Heart Hold

with meh dais, 128–30

with ring slings, 100–103

with stretchy wraps, 108–12

help, asking for, 138

i

I-Got-You-a-Present Swaddle, 57–59

Infantino, 93

k

Kinderpack, 90

K'tan, 83

l

The Let-It-Hang Swaddle, 35–37

LÍLLÉbaby, 90

m

meh dais (mei tais)

age range for, 91

back carrying with, 134

benefits of, 90–91

brands of, 93

buying, 92–93

description of, 91

Heart-to-Heart Hold, 128–30

locations for, 91

nonideal situations for, 91

smaller babies and, 91–92

wearing, 128–30

Moby, 83–84

Moro reflex, 13–14

M position, 74

n

Natibaby, 87

o

One Arm In, One Arm Out, 39–41

p

parents

survival tips for new, 136–37

swaddling for, 43

q

Quick-and-Easy Swaddle, 31–33

r

rail, 78

ring slings

age range for, 79

back carrying with, 133

benefits of, 79

brands of, 81

buying, 80–81

description of, 79

Heart-to-Heart Hold, 100–103

invention of, 72

locations for, 79

nonideal situations for, 79

Ring Sling Hip Carry, 104–6

wearing, 100–106

s

Sakura Bloom, 81

Sears, William, 72

SIDS (sudden infant death syndrome), 14, 15

skin-to-skin cuddling, 17, 19

sleeping

    amount of time for, 14, 19, 20

    co-, 16

    positions for, 14, 15, 21

    schedule for, 137–38

    swaddling and, 14, 16, 19

slings. *See* ring slings

soft structured carriers. *See* SSCs

Solly Baby, 84

SSCs (soft structured carriers)

    age range for, 88

    back carrying with, 134

    benefits of, 87, 88

    brands of, 89–90

    buying, 89

    description of, 87–88

    locations for, 88

    nonideal situations for, 88–89

    wearing facing in, 120–23

    wearing facing out, 124–27

startle reflex, 13–14

strollers, 70, 71

survival tips for new parents, 136–37

swaddling

    for adults, 43

    from baby's point of view, 42

    basics of, 16–17

    benefits of, 10, 13–15, 42

    blankets for, 16, 21

    excessive, 19–21

    history of, 15–16

    pitfalls for, 21

    safety and, 21

    sleep and, 14, 16, 19

    starting, 17

    stopping, 17–18

    taking a break from, 20

swaddling techniques

    Bathtime Swaddle, 49–51

    The Blowout Swaddle (sweatshirt), 45–47

    Can't-Break-Free Swaddle, 27–29

    Good-Enough-to Eat Swaddle, 23–25

    I-Got-You-a-Present Swaddle, 57–59

    The Let-It-Hang Swaddle, 35–37

One Arm In, One Arm Out, 39–41
Quick-and-Easy Swaddle, 31–33
Sweet Pea Swaddle, 61–63
Too-Tired-to-Care Swaddle, 53–55
swaying, 65
sweatshirt, swaddling with, 45–47
Sweet Pea Swaddle, 61–63

t
tail, 79
Too-Tired-to-Care Swaddle, 53–55
top rail, 78
traveling, 21

w
weight, gaining, 20
white noise, 64
WildBird, 81
wraps, stretchy
    age range for, 82
    back carrying with, 133–34
    benefits of, 81, 82
    brands of, 83

buying, 82–83
Heart-to-Heart Hold, 108–12
location for, 81
nonideal situations for, 82
wearing, 108–12
wraps, woven
    age range for, 85
    back carrying with, 134
    benefits of, 84, 85
    brands of, 87
    buying, 85–86
    description of, 84–85
    Front Wrap Cross Carry (FWCC), 86,
        114–19
    locations for, 85
    nonideal situations for, 85
    wearing, 114–19